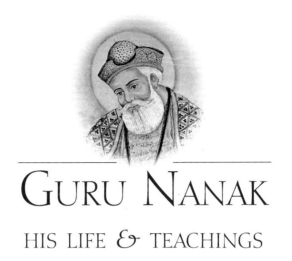

GURU NANAK

HIS LIFE & TEACHINGS

ROOPINDER SINGH

Rupa & Co

THIS BOOK IS FOR
GIANI GURDIT SINGH
MY FATHER, MY INSPIRATION

First Published 2004
Second Impression 2007

Published by
Rupa & Co
7/16, Ansari Road, Daryaganj
New Delhi 110 002

Sales Centres:
Allahabad Bangalore Chandigarh Chennai
Hyderabad Jaipur Kathmandu
Kolkata Mumbai Pune

Illustrations courtesy:
Government Museum and Art Gallery, Chandigarh;
Sikandar Singh Bhayee;
Giani Gurdit Singh's collection;
Chief Khalsa Diwan, Amritsar;
Himachal Pradesh Museum, Shimla;
Sardarni Malvinder Kaur;
Maps by KBK Infographics New Delhi.

Book design & typeset by
Arrt Creations
45 Nehru Apts, Kalkaji
New Delhi 110 019

Printed in India by
Gopsons Paper Ltd
A-14 Sector 60
Noida 201 301

(Pg ii): The opening folio of an illuminated manuscript of **Guru Granth Sahib**,
with the first lines of the **Japji** *inscribed in Gurmukhi script.*

Preface

Grateful and thankful. These words express, somewhat inadequately, my feelings as I write the preface of the second edition of the book which has been received so kindly by readers and scholars.

As I said earlier, any reader who picks up a copy of this book is justified in asking: "Why another book on Guru Nanak?" Some people write to dispense knowledge. I am in no position to make such claims. This book is a small window to the world of Guru Nanak Dev and his teachings, and there are many reasons why Guru Nanak needs to be read about and understood.

Guru Nanak founded the youngest religion in the world. Hinduism, Buddhism, Jainism, Christianity and Islam all predate Sikhism. The religion that he founded is studied as a discipline in many a university in India and abroad and his followers have made the world their home. Two per cent of the Canadians today are Sikhs.

The Guru's message was original and unambiguous. He, however, also reached out and interacted with saints of various persuasions, showing a remarkable openness when bigotry had closed the minds of people. He practised what he preached, and was willing to engage in dialogue with the learned, constantly enriching himself and the environment he was in.

At that time when the world was opening up, Guru Nanak spread his message by engaging the minds of thousands of people. He travelled to various sacred centres of pilgrimage that were important to Hindus and Muslims within India and abroad. He went to Baghdad and Mecca, both important Islamic centres of the time; visited important Hindu places of pilgrimage such as Kurukshetra, Hardwar and Jagannath Puri. He even climbed Mount Sumer (now called the Kailash Mountain) and held discussions with the *sidhs* (accomplished yogis) who had renounced the world.

One looks in wonder at how Guru Nanak revelled in meeting new people and exchanging ideas. The Guru came across the poor and the rich, saints and robbers. He interacted with the prevailing cultures even as he preached his new way. Guru Nanak did not hide behind the abstractions of mere metaphysics. Much of Guru Nanak's writing has references to contemporary events. While he drew upon various cultural metaphors in conveying his statements on the oneness of God and universal brotherhood, the message that he gave was unique in its depth and vision.

Anyone who has worked on Guru Nanak knows that while his compositions have been meticulously recorded, the same fidelity cannot be obtained from various biographical accounts, especially the Janamsakhis, which do not follow a strict chronological order, so beloved of the historian. That the Janamsakhis, which are placed by scholars in the early seventeenth century, are hagiographical accounts is stating the obvious, but the accounts therein have been tempered by the compositions of Bhai Gurdas (1544-1637), who gives an authoritative, though brief, account in his *Vars*.

What is being presented here is a simple account, which has been based both on scholarly works, most of which have been listed in the bibliography, and on absorbed oral tradition which is very much a part of a Sikh's life.

Visuals form a prominent part of this book because they enhance, in many ways, our understanding. There is no contemporary likeness of Guru Nanak that has survived. What we have are idealised renderings envisioning Guru Nanak. They were created about a century and a half after Guru Nanak in the style of Indian miniature then in vogue.

Most of the paintings of Guru Nanak and other Gurus are from the early eighteenth century and are stylised versions heavily influenced by various schools of art, such as *Pahari*, Sikh and Late Mughal. Many of the miniatures being reproduced in the book are from the family workshop of Nainsukh of Guler, who is described by Prof B. N. Goswamy, a leading authority on Indian art, as "a great Indian painter from a small hill-state." Prof Goswamy's work, especially in the area of *Pahari* painting, has deeply influenced modern scholarship, and I have been very fortunate in getting his guidance. The sketches in the book are, according to him, from a Guler series and were evidently used as master designs.

This series of sketches—all brush drawings on uncoloured paper—from the Guler family, and some paintings based on them, in opaque watercolour, are in the collection of the Government Museum and Art Gallery, Chandigarh. I am grateful to Mr V. N. Singh, Director of the museum, for his cooperation and help.

Another series of Janamsakhi paintings given in the book are dated Samvat 1781 (1860 AD), according to the colophon. These previously unpublished works which are in the Late Provincial Mughal style are from a Janamsakhi that is with the Bagrian family, which traces its roots back to the times of Guru Hargobind, the sixth Guru. They have been reproduced here through the courtesy of Sikandar Singh Bhayee.

Giani Gurdit Singh and Sardarni Inderjit Kaur, my parents, are both scholars and devout Sikhs. I have drawn heavily upon their generosity and help in many ways during the writing of the book. The patience of many friends who read the manuscript as it developed was also tested, and I am grateful for their advice and help. After the book was published, I received valuable input from readers and scholars who commented on various aspects of the book. I thank them, and I have incorporated their suggestions in this revised edition.

The illustration on the cover is from my personal collection. Many of the pictures used to illustrate the chapter on *Japji* are from the collection of Giani Gurdit Singh, who has spent the last sixty years researching manuscripts of *Guru Granth Sahib*.

The maps used in the book are based on the pioneering work done by Prof Fauja Singh and Prof Kirpal Singh in *Atlas: Travels of Guru Nanak*. It was published by Punjabi University, Patiala, in 1976, and has an introduction by my mother, who was then Vice-Chancellor of the university. I also gratefully acknowledge their pioneering work, and the help rendered by Vijay Kumar and Ramneek Singh from KBK Infographics, New Delhi, who have made the new maps.

Numismatics, or the study of coins, has its own impact on how history is perceived. All Sikh coins which remained in circulation from 1710 to 1856 were in the name of the Gurus and the Almighty. Sikh coins did not have any pictorial representation of the Gurus, though auspicious tokens did, and the book has some illustrations based on such tokens, both from my personal collection and that of Dr Surinder Singh, a keen Sikh numismatist.

The writing of this book has been a great learning experience for me. I hope that, to a certain extent, it has succeeded in making the life and the teaching of the founder of the Sikh religion more accessible, and in, hopefully, whetting the reader's appetite for more.

R. S.

The opening folio of another illuminated manuscript of Guru Granth Sahib.
It has the first lines of the Japji *inscribed in Gurmukhi script.*

GURU NANAK'S MESSAGE

*"There is no Hindu,
no Mussalman.
All are creatures
of God and
His creation."*

At Hardwar, Guru Nanak saw pilgrims who were ritualistically offering water to the east so that it would reach their ancestors in heaven. Seeing this age-old Hindu custom, Guru Nanak started offering water to the west. When asked what he was doing, he said he was sending water to his fields, a few hundred kilometres away. If the water they offered could reach the heavens, why could it not reach his fields, he asked.

At Mecca, Guru Nanak lay down to rest. He fell asleep and at some point, his feet happened to point in the direction of the Kaaba. A Qazi admonished Guru Nanak: "Who is this sleeping infidel? Why have you, O sinner, turned your feet towards God?" he said. To this Guru Nanak retorted: "Turn my feet in the direction where God is not."

Guru Nanak Dev, founder of the Sikh faith, used whatever methods needed: gentle persuasion, humour, sarcasm and even admonition to get his point across, as the instances given above show.

In the fifteenth century, medieval Indian society was divided into two distinct and mutually antagonistic religious groups—pan-Hinduism and Islam. These were by no means homogenous: within each group were distinct strands and various shades of persuasion. In such a milieu, Guru Nanak maintained: "There is no Hindu, no Mussalman. All are creatures of God and His creation." When the fight was "my way to my God" is better than "your way to your God," he declared that there was only one God, though there were many ways to reach Him.

While Buddhism and Jainism were independent religions, there were many divisions within the Hindu faith, the prominent being Vaishnavites, Shaivites and Nath Yogis. Then there were the various castes—Brahmin, Kshatriya, Vaish and Shudra—with interaction between those classified as the upper castes and the lower a taboo.

Islamic society, too, was not monochromatic. There were the traditional divisions between the Shias and the Sunnis, with the latter dominating the ruling class. An important Islamic tradition was that of the Sufis, who considered Allah to be immanent in the heart of the devotee. Their ritual practices included dancing, remembrance and recitation of Allah's name.

Guru Nanak came out strongly against all artificially created divisions and all discrimination, both in word and deed. "The caste of a person is what he does," he maintained and set out to dissolve differences through the institutions of *sangat* and *pangat*.

When Guru Nanak met the *Siddhs*, or holy men who had renounced the world, he was critical of them. To him, the life of a religious person was a life lived piously, in *toto*. Not for him was the luxury of an escape from the responsibilities of a householder. It was through good conduct and *Naam*, the recitation of the Name of the Lord, that his followers would attain *mukti* or the freedom from the endless cycle of life and death. The life of a mendicant was not for his followers. They had to participate in worldly affairs and take care of their family responsibilities and, above all, live as good human beings.

"Religion consists not of mere words. He who looks upon all men as equal is religious," says Guru Nanak. Universal brotherhood is a strong theme in Guru Nanak's *bani*, as is evident from the following: "O Nanak, the Master is such as unites everyone."[1] God, for the Guru, was the binding force, not a divisive "my" or "our" God. This God was not to be found in remote temples or far away places. He is immanent, thus found everywhere.

At a time when women were treated as inferior to men and impure, and it was said that you had to be born a man in order to attain *mukti*, Guru Nanak said the way to realisation of God was open for all human beings including women. He came out strongly against the "impure" label that was given to women. "Why revile her, of whom are born great ones of the earth," he says in *Guru Granth Sahib*, the holy book of the Sikhs.

1 *Guru Granth Sahib*, page 72.

India was then governed by the Mughals, whose rule was exploitative. This attitude percolated down to the officials who, whether Muslim or Hindu, treated common people as vassals. Guru Nanak strongly disapproved of the local administrative machinery when he said: "Greed and sin have become the king and the minister. Falsehood is the local governor. Lust is the deputy with whom consultations are held."

Hypocrisy, in all its hues, was a special focus of Guru Nanak's criticism. There is an interesting anecdote about his chiding a Qazi for thinking about a foal at home while praying, rather than concentrating on his prayers. Elsewhere, the Guru says: "We are good at talk, vicious in deeds. Our minds are black from within, though we are white from without."

The Guru also stressed on forgiveness as an essential of human interaction. He said: "Millions have perished for want of compassion and forbearance."[2] During his travels, called *udasis*, he often came across intolerant people whom he always forgave, all the while maintaining that it was stupid to entangle oneself with a foolish person.

Guru Nanak was concerned with ordinary people, and his compositions reflect the language of the people of his time. His words did not need any interpretation—though the import of what he said was profound.

Guru Granth Sahib contains 947 compositions of Guru Nanak's *bani*, his teachings. They have a universal appeal and provide answers to the myriad social and ethical problems we face today, and most probably will be facing tomorrow. The teachings of the Guru need to be studied carefully, but more than that, they ought to be assimilated so that they are reflected in our conduct. As the Guru says, education alone is not enough: "The educated should be reckoned ignorant if he shows greed and ego."[3]

The compositions of Guru Nanak contain truths that pertain not only to the religious aspect of our lives, but also social and family matters, things that have been ordinarily considered outside the purview of religion.

Guru Nanak founded Sikhism in a land where there were already two well-established ancient religions, Hinduism and Islam. However, with the passage of time, their original form had been corrupted. The Guru gave the world a simple, non-ritualistic religion that allows its followers to live a spiritual life while taking care of their worldly duties.

---

2 *Guru Granth Sahib*, page 937.
3 *Guru Granth Sahib*, page 140.

While there is no contemporary physical representation of Guru Nanak, we know that he wore a *chola* or a cloak, and wooden sandals. He wore a *seili* and a *topi* (a skein of twisted woollen thread and a cap) to cover his head. There still exists a *rudraksha mala* that he is said to have worn, and certain other personal effects that are lovingly maintained by the descendants of the people who the Guru gave these items to.

Guru Nanak has been erroneously called a product of the Bhakti Movement. His influence on many of the *bhagats* of the movement is evident from the transformation that we see in their writings. The concept of God evolved from *Sargun* (God in visible forms) in their earlier writings to *Nirgun* (the formless God) in the later ones. The compositions of fifteen such *bhagats*[4] have been incorporated in *Guru Granth Sahib*.

Unlike the *bhagats*, Guru Nanak was the only person of his time who founded a religion, had his *bani* written and edited in his presence, and set up *sangats* to propagate his teachings. He set up a community at Kartarpur, which became a focal point for the new religion, giving it an anchor. Today there are twenty-three million Sikhs the world over who revere the founder of their faith and follow the basic dictum: *Kirat karo, wand chhako, nam japo,* i.e., engage in honest labour, share what you have and recite the Name of God.

4 The names of the bhagats and the number (in brackets) of their compositions included in the *Guru Granth Sahib* are as follows: Kabir (534), Farid (123) Namdev (62) Ravidas (40), Surdas (2), Sain (1), Sadhna (1), Jaidev (2), Trilochan (5), Dhanna (4), Parmanand (1), Peepa (1) Beini (3), Bhikhan (2) and Ramanand (1). Source Giani Gurdit Singh.

opposite page:
Guru Nanak Dressed in an Inscribed Robe: Watercolour on machine-made paper. Punjab, last quarter of nineteenth century.

A GURU IS BORN

*"He will sit under a canopy.
Both Hindus and Turks will
revere him…
he will worship and
acknowledge none but One
Formless Lord and teach
others to do so…."*

Scholars generally agree that Guru Nanak was born in the middle of
the month of Baisakh, according to the Indian calendar, which works
out to April 15, 1469, in the more commonly used Gregorian
calendar. He was born to Kalu Bedi and Tripta in the early hours of
the morning at Rai Bhoen di Talwandi,[5] a village now in
Sheikhupura district of Pakistan, sixty-five kilometers west of Lahore.
The birthday, however, is traditionally celebrated on the full-moon
night of the Indian month of *Kartik*, which falls in October/
November.[6]

Kalu Bedi was a *patwari,* a revenue official, in the village, thus, a
socially prominent person. His wife, Tripta, came from a village called
Chahal, which was near Lahore, the cultural and administrative
capital of Punjab at that time.

Soon after the birth, Kalu consulted, as custom dictated, the
village pandit, Hardyal, on the newly arrived baby's horoscope to

---

5 It is now known as Nankana Sahib. Gurdwara Janamasthan marks the birth place
of Guru Nanak. Other prominent *gurdwaras* there include Gurdwara Bal Lila and
Gurdwara Kiara Sahib. See map on page 13.
6 Almost all the books on Guru Nanak accept April as the month of his birth. The
date is April 15, 1469, which is given in *Puratan Janaksakhis* and the *Meharban
Janamsakhi.* As early as in 1912, Karam Singh, a Sikh scholar of repute, wrote a
book titled *Kartik ke Baisakh* (November or April) in which he marshalled the
arguments about Guru Nanak's birth being in mid-Baisakh. Even though the date
of birth is accepted in April, it has traditionally been celebrated in November and
the adoption of the Nanakshahi Calendar by the SGPC in 2003 has further
strengthened this tradition.

opposite page:
Pandits greet baby Nanak's parents.

detail:
Kalu Bedi and Mata Tripta take their
son to Pandit Hardyal.

find out what his future held for him. "He will sit under a canopy. Both Hindus and Turks will revere him…he will worship and acknowledge none but One Formless Lord and teach others to do so…. Every creature he will consider as God's creation. O Kalu, this will be my grief that I may not live to see the glory that will be his. Who knows how long I will live?"[7]

Pandit Hardyal felicitated the family and said he would return after thirteen days to give a name to the child. He called the child Nanak and said that just as the name was common between the Hindus and the Muslims, the child would not distinguish between the two when he grew up.

At that time Bahlol Lodhi (1451-1498), an Afghan, ruled from Delhi. He had considerably revived the power and prestige of the Sultanate of Delhi, but had succeeded to a throne historically associated with the names of Alauddin Khilji and Muhammad bin Tughlaq. His kingdom was a pale shadow of what their kingdoms had been.

opposite page:
Young Nanak brought to the school by his
father, Kalu Bedi.

7 Bala Janamsakhi.

The father takes the young Nanak to Pandha Gopal for schooling. opposite page: Detail.

The society, on the whole, was divided into Muslims, who constituted the ruling class, and the Hindus, who were the subjects despite their being the majority. Even these were not homogenous groups: among the Muslims, there were differences between the 'immigrants' and the natives, or converted Muslims. Similarly, there were many distinctions among the Hindus.

However, the interaction between the two classes was minimal and functional and the Hindus were discriminated against. A major example is the infamous *jiziya,* the tax on non-Muslims, which was imposed by most of the Mughal emperors. Even those who did not impose it, did not abolish this tax either. It arose out of the notion that non-Muslims living in an Islamic state would have to pay for the privilege. It also imposed a series of restrictions on such subjects. Slavery also existed, though the relationship between the slave and the master was not quite as bad as it was in certain other countries at that time.

Overall, it was an agrarian society in which violent invasions punctuated relatively long periods of peace. Most towns had Muslim populations and justice was administered by *qazis,* Muslim priests, in accordance with Islamic precepts. Local governance was in the hands of revenue officials, the senior ones being Afghans, and the junior, more experienced ones, being drawn from the native Hindu population.

As a child, Nanak led a life much like that of other children. He played with children of his age and frolicked around. However, unlike many children, he was wont to share all that he had, like goodies to eat, with his sister and friends. He was also different in that he loved to meet various holy men, the *fakirs, yogis* and monks travelling through Talwandi.

When Nanak was five years old, his father sent him to Pandha[8] Gopal to study. The child learned elementary education with an emphasis on language and arithmetic. While he did not make much progress in learning his ancestral vocation of maintaining ledgers and accounts, his poetic expression of lofty thoughts impressed Pandha Gopal.

A major development in young Nanak's life was the marriage of his elder sister Nanaki at an early age, as was the custom . She was married to Jairam, son of Parmanand Palta, a minister. The match had been arranged by Rai Bular, the local landlord, who was also a friend of the family. Bular was very fond of the young Nanak.

After her marriage, Nanaki moved to Sultanpur Lodhi, where her husband worked as an official for the local government. Sultanpur was then a thriving commercial centre, a major venue of Islamic learning and a provincial administrative headquarter *(shiq).*

8 Pandha is a colloquialism for Upadhyaya, which is Sanskrit for scholar.

Nanaki was Nanak's confidante, a person from whom he received the greatest understanding and affection, and who saw in Nanak a *persona extraordinaire*. She was five years his elder and had played a major role in raising him. The two were very close. While Nanak was happy that his sister was getting married, he also felt sad at being separated from his sibling, who had been there to hold his hand through the trials and tribulations of childhood and teens.

The change in Nanak, after his sister left for her new home, was noticeable—he appeared sad and withdrawn. It was obvious that he was distracted and this reflected in both his studies as well as the tasks assigned to him by his father. While the teacher continued to hope that Nanak would develop an inclination for accounting and similar subjects, the pupil composed the following:

> Make your ink by burning up worldly attachments
> And pounding the ashes to powder;
> Let pure mind be your prayer.

Make love your pen, and your heart the writer,
And write as your Guru instructs.
Write you His name and His praises.
Write that He is without limit and fathomless.
This is the writing, this the account
One ought to learn
This will be one's true credit
Here and hereafter.[9]

This composition is enshrined in *Guru Granth Sahib*. The young Nanak continued his studies with Pandha Gopal. Soon the teacher recommended a Sanskrit scholar for his ward because of Nank's spiritual inclinations.

Pandit Brijlal, known to be a brilliant teacher as well as spiritually blessed, was requested to teach the child, which he did for two years. This exposed the young Nanak to the traditional learning contained in Sanskrit classics. But the spiritual restlessness in him was not quenched. Very soon, the Pandit declared that Nanak "had nothing more to learn from him and that Nanak was an embodiment of sacred wisdom. Everyday his classmates squatted around him to listen to his melodious songs, fascinating stories, and discourses."

Qutab-ud-Din, a local maulvi, was then engaged to teach Persian and Arabic to Nanak. Within two years, Nanak was proficient enough in the two languages to study their literature. His use of Koranic metaphors in his later compositions indicates that he had studied the holy text well, just as he had Hindu scriptures. His early association with the family of a Muslim neighbour is also credited with enhancing his inborn egalitarianism, and it must have been unusual, since interaction at the level of families of adherents of different religions was almost unheard of in those days.

Kalu wanted his son to become worldly-wise. So he set him tasks that required practical responsibilities, one of which entailed Nanak's taking out the family's livestock for grazing in the fields nearby. This was a convenient arrangement for the young Nanak, as it gave him a lot of solitude which allowed him to contemplate. This also gave him the opportunity to meet a variety of mendicants and fakirs who frequented the jungles around Talwandi, and discuss diverse aspects of spirituality with them. There are different accounts of unusual

---

9 No doubt translation is like seeing the reverse of embroidery, but an attempt has been made to convey the lofty thoughts in a simple manner. The writer has consulted a number of sources for the translation of various *shabads* from *Gurbani* or the sacred writing of the Sikh Gurus. He has also drawn on his own interpretations where necessary in order to simplify/clarify the text beyond mere linguistic translation. The writer is quite conscious of not being able to fully capture the beauty of the original text, and apologises for inadequacies that are still there, despite best efforts.

Map of Nankana Sahib

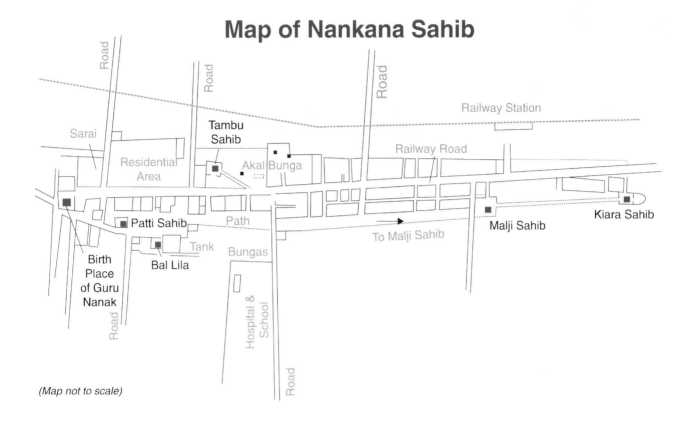

(Map not to scale)

happenings and miracles that took place during those excursions and of how people were astounded by them. Some of them are narrated in various *janamsakhis*[10].

As Nanak reached the age of thirteen, it was time for him to be given the *janeu*, the sacred thread woven of seven cotton strings and worn by upper-caste Hindus as a mark of their being 'twice-born'. Elaborate arrangements were made for the occasion and relatives and friends were invited. But when Pandit Hardyal, the family priest, tried to place the thread across Nanak's shoulders, as is usually done, the young Nanak refused to wear it, saying: "How can you differentiate between men by such badges ('twice-born')? It is their actions that should characterise them. I will not take such a badge. Besides, the thread will get soiled and break."

Nanak's steadfast refusal to wear the sacred thread took his parents and the guests by surprise, but he recited the following hymn elucidating what a *janeu* ought to be:

> Let compassion be your cotton!
> Spin it into the yarn of contentment;
> Give it knots of continence,
> And the twist of truth,
> Thus will you make a *janeu* for the soul.

10 *Janmsakhis* are hagiographic life stories of the Gurus. They date back to the seventeenth century and are among the earliest sources of information on the Gurus. The main *janamsakhis* are *Puratan, Meharban* and *Bala*.

If such a one you have,
Put it on me.
The thread so made will neither snap, nor become soiled.
It will neither be burned nor lost.
Blessed is the man, O Nanak,
Who wears such a thread around his neck![11]

The ceremony did not conclude and the assembled guests left. Obviously the family must have been upset, too, since elaborate arrangements had been made for the guests.

It is with the fakirs that another popular parable of adolescent Nanak is associated. Kalu gave him twenty-one silver coins and asked him to invest the sum usefully. Nanak was expected to go to the nearby town of Chuharkana and purchase certain goods that could be sold at a profit in his own village. Bala, a friend of Nanak, was assigned to be his escort.

detail:
An adolescent Nanak meets sadhus *of the Nirbani sect. He later used up the money given to him by his father for trade to feed the hungry sadhus.*

11 *Guru Granth Sahib*, page 471.

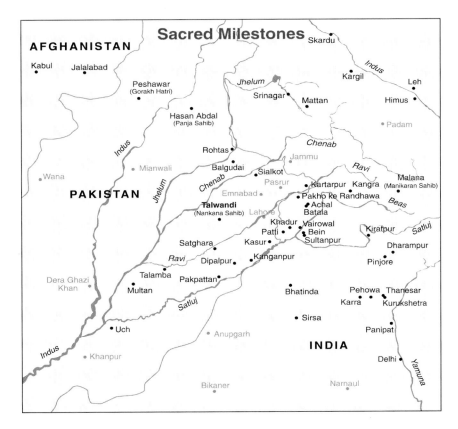

On his way, Nanak met some *sadhus*[12] from the Nirbani sect, who were in various stages of meditation. Some were reciting religious texts, others had their arms raised, and still others who would not sit down. The leader of the *sadhus*, responding to Nanak's query, said they had not eaten for days, and would eat only when God sent food for them.

After spending time with them, Nanak continued on his journey to Chuharkana, where he bought food and provisions. On his return journey, he gave all the groceries to the *sadhus*. In his reckoning he had spent the money usefully, but his father did not agree. He was remonstrated by his father, although Nanak remained convinced that he had done the right thing.

In the meantime it transpired that Nanak's sister Nanaki was missing him. So she and her husband Jairam invited him to Sultanpur. Kalu approved of this and, thus, the preparations for the journey were made.

Before he left his ancestral village and his mother's protective, benevolent bosom, there was an elaborate farewell in which Nanak's friends, including Mardana, took part. Mardana was to become his life-long companion and accompany him on his travels. Mardana was a Muslim *doom*, a professional singer. In hindsight, the significance of the farewell is heightened since Nanak was never to live in this village again but only to visit it from time to time.

12 Naga Sadhus, literally naked saints who have renounced everything, are a particular sect among the Hindus.

REVELATION

"The secret of religion is in living in the world without being overcome by it."

That Nanak's first journey was to be to his sister's house was indeed full of meaning. It was she who had recognised his genius and, along with her mother, given him the nurturing that allowed his inner genius and unconventional being to blossom.

When Nanak, accompanied by Bala, reached Sultanpur after a five-day journey, his sister touched his feet in reverence. Nanak stopped her, saying that she was elder to him, and it was his duty to touch her feet. But Nanaki replied: "This would be true if you were an earthly being."[13]

Jairam was also very happy to meet Nanak, and soon got him a job as in-charge of the granaries and stores of the local chieftain, Shiqdar Daulat Khan. Given his reputation, like the incident when he had spent his father's money to feed the hungry *sadhus*, there was some concern about how Nanak would undertake his duties. This proved unfounded as he was diligent and conscientious in executing his responsibilities. Nanak lived by what he said: "The secret of religion is in living in the world without being overcome by it."

Nanak's day would start with a bath in Bein, a small rivulet flowing nearby, followed by meditation and contemplation of His *Naam.* He would dispense the goods which were often given as salaries to the employees of the Nawab. He would also distribute a part of his salary to the needy.

By this time, Nanaki wanted to find a bride for Nanak. She brought up the matter with her husband, and he got in touch with Mula Chana, a fellow *Khatri* and also a *patwari* of Pakho ke Randhawa. He had a daughter of marriageable age. After both the respective fathers had approved, it was time for the wedding ceremonies. It entailed a five-day journey to the bride Sulakhni's

Young Nanak conversing with his brother-in-law, Jairam.
opposite page:
A group of holy men with offerings for Guru Nanak.

---

13 *Bala Janamsakhi.*

Nanak gets a job as in charge of the granaries and stores of Shiqdar Daulat Khan at Sultanpur.

right:
Nanak distributing goods from the stores to the poor at Sultanpur.

parents' house. The *barat* (wedding party) spent three days there and came back to Sultanpur after the marriage was solemnised.[14]

Sulakhni was a gentle and virtuous bride who built a happy and hospitable home in Sultanpur. A son was born to the couple in 1494 and was named Srichand. Right from childhood, this child was attracted to spiritual matters. He lived the life of an ascetic and in his later life became the founder of the Udasi sect which still has *deras* in many parts of northern India.

Nanak and Sulakhni's younger son, Lakhmidas, was born in 1496. He married and raised a family.[15] Nanak lived a simple life. He worked during the day and in the evening there used to be a gathering of people around him who would sing hymns composed by him and discuss spiritual matters. This was the foundation of the concept of *sangat*, which is now the bedrock of Sikh religious tradition.

14 Today there stands a beautiful gurdwara at the spot where the wedding took place on 24 Jeth 1544 (according to Bhai Kahn Singh's *Mahankosh*), and it is celebrated annually as a festival in August.
15 His descendants live in various parts of the country, with the seat being at Dehra Baba Nanak. The current scion of the family is Baba Sarabjot Singh Bedi, who lives in Una, Himachal Pradesh.

One day when Nanak went for his customary morning ablutions, he did not return. He reappeared after a gap of three days, during which he had a spiritual experience, a communion with God. *Puratan Janamsakhi* describes it thus:

> As the Lord willed, Nanak the devotee was escorted to His Presence. Then a cup filled with *amrit* (nectar) was given to him with the command: "Nanak, this is the cup of Name-adoration. Drink it...I am with you and I do bless and exalt you. Whoever remembers you will have My favour. Go, rejoice in My Name and teach others the Name-adoration.... I have bestowed on you My name. Let this be your calling." Nanak made the salutation and stood up.

Guru Nanak remained silent even after people found him and his first public utterance was:

> "There is no Hindu, no Mussalman."

The wedding procession of Nanak going to Pakho ke Randhawa.

Another *janamsakhi* says that Guru Nanak emerged from the rivulet Bein and enunciated the *Sodar* at this time. This *bani* that occurs thrice in *Guru Granth Sahib*, is a paean of divine laudation. It describes the vision of His presence:

opposite page:
The marriage ceremony of Guru Nanak.

How wondrous is Your portal, How wondrous Your abode, Oh Lord

From where You look after all Your creation

Countless the melodies, innumerable the minstrels too,

Countless notes and measures adore You with celestial minstrels drawing in harmony.

Air, Fire and Water, all adore you,

Dharamraj, too, pays homage to you,

(In fulfilment of Your Will, O Lord) Chitragupt records human actions,

For Dharamraj to adjudge thereon.

Ishar, Brahma, and Vishnu, all created and graced by You.

Bows to You, Lord Indra from his seat

With host of deities around

Sing Your praises, ascetics in trance, holy men too meditate on You

Men of continence, charity and poise,

All chant Your praises, as do valiant heroes.

Scholars of Vedas and great sages have all exalted You through all ages

So do bewitching ladies in heaven, earth and nether world

By the fourteen gems that You did create, by Hindu pilgrimages all sixty-eight,

By warriors ever valiant in strife

By all sources from where came life (egg, womb, sweat or seed)

Your name is ever glorified.

So all regions, continents, and the entire universe,

Propped on Your support

Only such are inspired to Lord You

As win Your pleasure.

Innumerable more, beyond my reckoning, sing Your praises, O Lord, says Nanak.

Eternal You are, O Lord of Universe!

Ever True is Your name

You who has created this universe,

Having created beings of diverse species and shades

You look after Your handicraft

As flowing from Your own grace.

It all comes to pass

As it pleases You

None may meddle with Your decree

King of Kings You are, O Lord

May I always abide by Your Will.[16]

16 Extracted from Japji, pauri 27.

SPREADING THE WORD

He decided to take along Mardana, the rabab *player who was his constant companion and friend, on these journeys.*

Now Guru Nanak knew that he had to spread his message as far and wide as he could. Thus, he decided to travel extensively.

He knew that he had to undertake this divine mission. He decided to take along Mardana, the *rabab* player who became his constant companion and friend, on these journeys. Guru Nanak sent Mardana to Bharoana, a village now in Kapurthala district of Punjab, to get a rabab from Tarindar, a master instrument maker. Much of the area he was planning to go through was uncharted. There was the danger of wild beasts and major physical threats in the form of thugs, dacoits, and other outlaws who waylaid travellers.

Besides these dangers, this was, in any case, an arduous undertaking, since for most of the time the Guru and his companion were travelling on foot. They survived on what they found or received, not on what they carried with them.

There are references in *Puratan Janamsakhi* to four others, i.e. Hassu Lohar, Shhian Chheemba, Saido Jat, and Tan Sukh Bania, who were among those who accompanied Guru Nanak and took down his *bani* during his travels.

Before embarking on this first journey, Guru Nanak first set things in order so that his family would be looked after in his absence. He bid farewell to his wife, sister and brother-in-law, said goodbye to his sons and set out on the first of his four major travels, called *udasis*, that were to take up the next twenty-three years of his life. His elder son, Srichand, was left in the care of Nanaki and Jai Ram, who did not have any child, and the younger, Lakhmidas, went with his mother to her ancestral home.

Then, dressed in garments that were composites of those worn by people of various faiths,[17] Guru Nanak set forth from Sultanpur for his first major travel.

Guru Nanak sends Mardana to fetch a rabab *from Pheranda (Pheru Rababi).*

opposite page:
Guru Nanak meets Malik Bhago and impresses upon him the merit of honest living.

17 Hindus and Muslims wear different traditional dresses. Even if the dress is similar, it will have variations that will allow a practiced eye to slot the person by his faith.

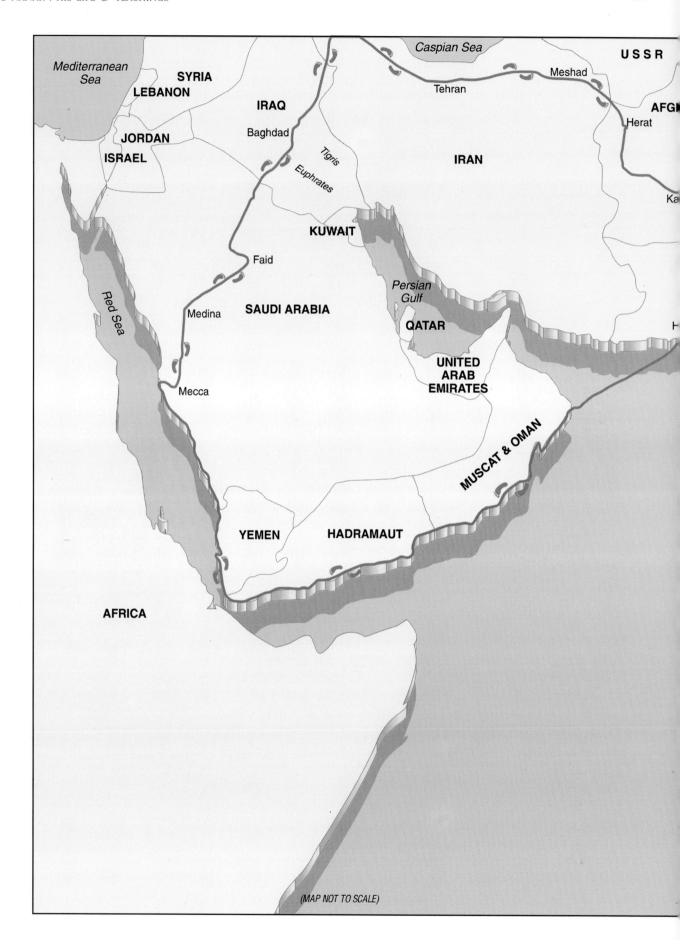

(MAP NOT TO SCALE)

Spreading the Word

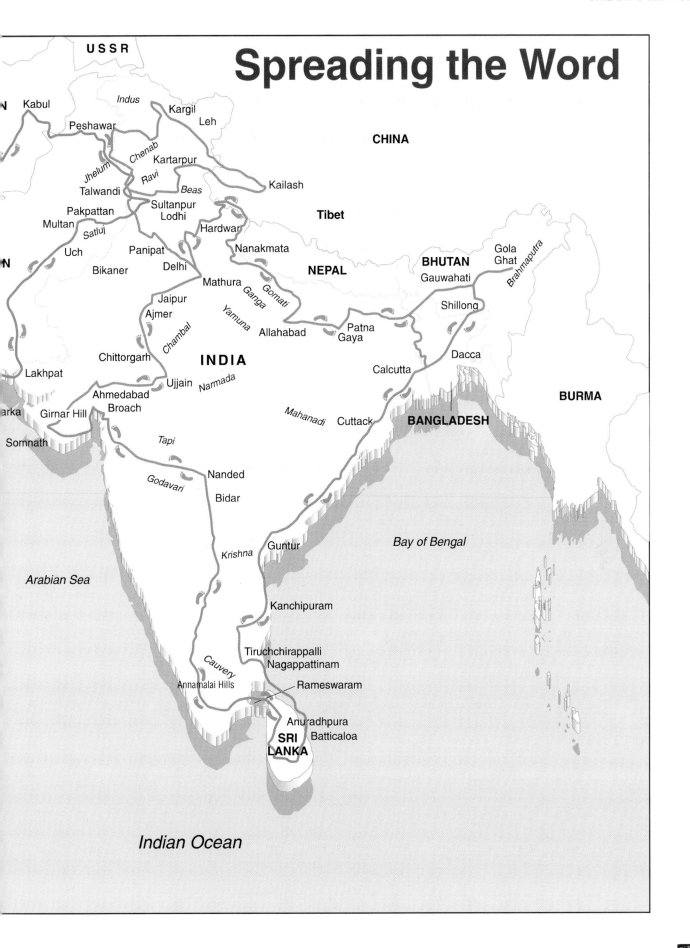

USSR

Kabul
Indus
Kargil
Leh
Peshawar
CHINA
Chenab
Kartarpur
Jhelum
Ravi
Kailash
Talwandi
Beas
Pakpattan
Sultanpur
Tibet
Lodhi
Multan
Satluj
Hardwar
Uch
Panipat
Nanakmata
Gola
Bikaner
Delhi
Ghat
BHUTAN
NEPAL
Brahmaputra
Gauwahati
Mathura
Gomati
Jaipur
Ganga
Shillong
Ajmer
Yamuna
Patna
Chambal
Allahabad
Gaya
INDIA
Chittorgarh
Dacca
Calcutta
Lakhpat
Ujjain
Narmada
Ahmedabad
BURMA
Broach
Mahanadi
Cuttack
arka
Girnar Hill
BANGLADESH
Somnath
Tapi

Nanded
Godavari
Bidar

Bay of Bengal

Krishna
Guntur

Arabian Sea

Kanchipuram

Tiruchchirappalli
Cauvery
Nagappattinam
Annamalai Hills
Rameswaram
Anuradhpura
SRI
Batticaloa
LANKA

Indian Ocean

THE FIRST JOURNEY:
THE SKY IS
THE SALVER

*Guru Nanak told his parents
that he had to leave them and
follow God's commandment.*

It was in 1496[18] that Guru Nanak, along with Mardana, left Sultanpur to deliver the world *(jagat udharan)* and spread the word about the Oneness of God.

They first visited Lahore and then went on to Talwandi, where he met his ageing parents who were very glad to see him. Rai Bular, the first to recognise the light of divinity in Guru Nanak and forever his well-wisher, also met the Guru. Mardana too visited members of his family in Talwandi.

After a few days' stay, Guru Nanak told his parents that he had to leave them and follow God's commandment. He went north-west, and after a distance of about sixty miles, reached Saidpur. [19]

Here he visited the house of Lalo, a carpenter, and the happenings there are narrated in traditional writings as follows:

> At Saidpur, he put up at the house of a carpenter named Lalo. The strange combination of a so-called Khatri saint with a low-caste Muslim minstrel, living and dining with a Hindu *Shudra*, became the subject of common talk. Mere gossip turned into severe criticism when Guru Nanak refused to participate in a grand feast given by Malik Bhago, a Hindu official of the local Pathan *faujdar*.

---

18 Bala *Janamsakhi.*
19 According to the Gujranwala District Gazetteer, 1935, page 354, Syedpur was colloquially corrupted to Saidpur. It is now called Eminabad and is in Gujranwala district in Pakistan.

opposite page:
Sajjan hears Guru Nanak's bani *sung by Mardana.*

Guru Nanak with Bhai Lalo at Saidpur.

The Guru was called by the Malik who remonstrated with him for preferring to dine with a low-caste carpenter and refusing to accept the invitation of a high-caste man like himself.

The Guru sent for a roti each from the sumptuous feast of the Malik as well as from the house of his poor host. Holding one in each hand, he said that he saw wholesome milk coming from the honestly earned bread of Lalo and the red blood of tortured humanity from the rich dainties of Malik Bhago. "I recognise no caste," he said. "There is only one brotherhood, that of humanity, and only one pollution, that of separateness, which is the root of all divisive notions that do not permit us to see our fellow beings of different denominations and persuasions without vision coloured with bias and prejudice.[20] Realisation dawned upon Malik Bhago and he became a changed man.

The fruits of honest labour are better than those of ill-gotten wealth. It was by such demonstrations that Guru Nanak showed the way to the people who had allowed artificial barriers between fellow beings to obscure the truth about the unity of mankind and honest living.

His travels then took him to Tulamba[21], a town on the banks of the river Ravi. This was an important town between Lahore and Multan. However, there was no official rest house. Private premises had been built to take care of both Hindu and Muslim travellers by a person called Shaikh Sajjan, who pretended to be pious.

Sajjan had lined the road to his private *dharamshala,* or rest house, with earthen pots filled with cool water for the travellers. They were even duly demarcated keeping religious sensibilities in mind. His *dharamshala* had a mosque as well as a mandir.

Sajjan would take good care of his guests, but later would kill them and rob them of their belongings. He would have done the same with Guru Nanak, but was attracted to the *kirtan,* or the holy hymns, recited by Guru Nanak to the accompaniment of the *rabab*[22] played by Mardana.

---

20 *A Short History of the Sikhs* by Principal Teja Singh.

21 Tulamba was a nodal town between Lahore and Multan. It is now called Makhdumpur and is in Multan district, Pakistan.

22 A *rabab* or a rebeck, which is a pear-shaped, two-stringed or three-stringed medieval instrument, is played with pluck. It was predominantly used in Afghanistan and India. There is evidence that this instrument may be the progenitor of a number of Indian instruments. The *sarinda, sarod,* and the *sarangi* are the most common derivatives of this instrument. At first, it may seem hard to make the connection between a plucked instrument and a bowed instrument. However, notice the "waist" in the middle of the *rabab,* which is an indication that the instrument at some time was played with a bow. All bowed instruments must be narrow at the place where the bow must pass. *Source*: David Courtney, a musician.

Guru Nanak said that the bright and lustrous copper utensils make a cloth inky black when rubbed, even if you wash them a hundred times. A *sajjan*, or friend, is a companion who renders help instantaneously when required. Beautiful buildings of various kinds are of little good if they are crumpled and deserted. Lovely white storks look wonderful when seen at various holy places, but they have only one mission, that of picking up small creatures and swallowing them! Only by reciting the Name of God would one be able to free oneself from eternal bondage.[23]

Sajjan felt that he had been accurately dissected by Guru Nanak, who had seen through his elaborate charade. Having seen himself in this light, and overwhelmed by the effect of the Guru's compositions, Sajjan confessed to his evil deeds.

The Guru made Sajjan donate his ill-gotten wealth to various people, and forgave him. Sajjan thereafter became a true friend of weary travellers and took care of them at his *dharamshala*, simultaneously disseminating the teachings of Guru Nanak. The tomb of Sajjan exists even today in Makhdumpur, in Pakistan.

Another significant incident[24] occurred during his visit to Kurukshetra. Venison, brought by a disciple of the Guru, was cooked. This act displeased the Brahmins among those present. Guru Nanak explained: "It is not easy to tell who sins—he who eats flesh or he who excludes flesh from his diet. They who foreswear flesh and hold their noses when near it might have no qualm about devouring their fellowmen under the cover of darkness….Those uninstructed in truth eat what they should not and eat not what they should." [25] Thus, the Guru highlighted the futility of attributing piety to consumption or non-consumption of a particular food.

Guru Nanak then spent time in Panipat and Delhi before reaching Hardwar. Another significant incident, briefly described in the beginning of the book, finds mention in oral tradition. It is said that he stood at a spot considered sacred on the banks of the Ganges and started offering water with cupped hands towards the west. When pilgrims, who were ritualistically throwing water to the east, curiously asked him why he was doing it in the opposite direction, Guru Nanak replied that he was throwing water towards his farm in Punjab, which needed to be irrigated. "But how can you expect the water to reach so far?" they asked. The Guru said to them: "If you are throwing water towards the east, expecting that it would reach your forefathers' spirits somewhere in heaven, surely

Guru Nanak meets Sajjan at Tulamba.

23 *Guru Granth Sahib*, page 129.
24 It is mentioned in *Bala Janamsakhi*.
25 *Guru Granth Sahib*, page 1289

my farm is nearer than where the forefathers are." Such incidents made people rethink about established customs that had become mere rituals and formed the core of religions practised in those days.

The high-caste Brahmins of the time would often draw a circle and cook food within it. People of low caste who were treated as pariahs were not allowed to even walk by the circle lest their shadow falls on the food being cooked, thereby 'defiling' it. One composition of Guru Nanak points out how the state of defilement is internal, not dependent on any outside influences. In a composition in *Sri Rag*, he says: "The real pariahs are the evil thoughts, cruelty, slander and wrath. It avails no one to draw circles around himself if these four were seated next to him. Let your demarcations be of truth, self-restraint and good acts and your ablutions the remembrance of His name. They alone shall be reckoned holy who lend not their steps to sin."

Generally commenting on disputes regarding what to eat and what not, Guru Nanak says: "Friend, eating that which causes discomfort to the body and makes the mind impure is forbidden."[26] Thus, he says that one can eat any kind of normal food, provided it is conducive to the body and the mind.

Guru Nanak with Mardana then went to a place called Gorakhmata, near Pilibhit, in Uttar Pradesh. Here lived a monastic order of Nath yogis. These yogis intimidated the locals as much by their abrasive and aloof behaiour as supernatural powers. They treated Mardana in their usual disdainful manner, but after they met Guru Nanak, they invited him to join their order. The Guru refused, saying that religion did not lie in renunciation, deprivation, or in empty words, but in being able to live an uncontaminated life amid worldly temptations. His message went home and many of the local people became Guru Nanak's followers and eventually Gorakhmata came to be known as Nanakmata.

After that, Guru Nanak was in Ayodhya during the festival of Diwali. It is associated with the return of Lord Rama to this ancient city. He mingled with thinkers and philosophers of various persuasions as well as common people who had gathered for the celebrations, interacting with the prevailing culture and preaching his new way.

Guru Nanak then went to Allahabad, which is historically called Prayag. Located at the confluence of the rivers Ganga, Yamuna and the subterranean Saraswati, Prayag has been considered a holy place since time immemorial. The Guru reached the town on a day considered auspicious by devotees for bathing in the river to expiate their sins.

While people were 'washing their sins' by bathing in the river,

26 *Ibid*, page 16.

Guru Nanak did not bathe in the river. This led to some confusion and a helpful priest pointed out to him that the auspicious time for the bath was passing by. "How would washing the body clean the sins of the heart?" the Guru asked, stressing that the purity of heart was only possible among those who kept the Lord in their minds and reflected his teachings in their actions.

There is another interesting story connected with Guru Nanak's visit to Pataliputra, which is now known as Patna. Once, when Mardana said that he was hungry, the Guru allowed him to go to the town and get something to eat. Mardana went to the jewellers' market where he was greeted by Adhrakha who was an assistant of Salis Rai, a prominent jeweller of the area and well regarded for his piety.

Adhrakha, at the bidding of his master, gave some food and money to Mardana. When Mardana went to Guru Nanak, the latter told him to return the money. When this was done, Salis Rai, accompanied by Adhrakha, carrying a basket of fruits and other presents, came to meet the Guru. The Guru told him that in matters of spiritual growth, temporal equations did not matter. What mattered was, not having more wealth, but having a rich soul. Though Salis Rai was wealthy and pious, the Guru said it was Adhrakha who

Guru Nanak in Kurukshetra during the solar eclipse.

was near spiritual realisation because of being blessed by God! Salis Rai realised the truth in Guru Nanak's words and, thereafter, he and Adhrakha took it upon themselves to carry on the mission of spreading the teachings of the Guru after Guru Nanak and Mardana left the city. Their descendants and the *sangat* of the area later met Guru Nanak's successors.*

Guru Nanak is also known to have visited Assam, which was then deemed as the land of sorceresses. Historian Himadri Banerjee says that Guru Nanak went to Kamrup around 1508. "He came with a disciple, Bhai Mardana, to the female-dominated land. At first, they were made to go through a lot of hardship. The magic and charms of the area were well known. It is said Queen Nur Shah cast her spell and turned Mardana into a ram. But the *sakhi* literature reveals that the hostility did not last long. She eventually recognised Guru Nanak's greatness and became his disciple."[27]

Guru Nanak went from Dhubri to Guwahati and Manipur. He continued south, travelling through Imphal and Dhaka, places which are marked by historic gurdwaras.

From Dhaka, Guru Nanak proceeded by sea to Puri, the ancient holy city of the Hindus. One of his most beautiful *banis* was composed in Puri. The Guru loved the clear sky with twinkling stars and the soft moonlight reflecting on the waves even as the wind played with them. All these and the sight of *aarti* (adoration), the Hindu rite of lighting the lamps and worshipping God, created the setting for one of his most beautiful compositions—*Aarti*. The Guru reminded the faithful that the cosmic *aarti* of the Eternal is ever being performed and needs to be reflected upon. It is there all the time and everywhere. He sang in *Raag Dhanasari*:

> The sky is the salver
> And the sun and the moon the lamps.
> The luminous stars on the heavens are the pearls.
> Scented air from the sandal-clad hills is the incense,
> The winds make a whisk for you,
> And the vast forests wreaths of flowers.
> The unstuck music is the trumpet.
> Thus goes on the *aarti* for you,
> O you dispeller of doubt and fear.[28]

---

*Fateh Chand Maini, a descendent of Salis Rai, was a prominent disciple of Guru Gobind Singh, the tenth Guru.

27 *The Other Sikhs: A View from Eastern India*, by Himadri Banerjee. He, however, has failed to find an echo of the Punjabi sources in contemporary Assamese history or literature. Guru Tegh Bahadur, the ninth Guru, visited Dhubri and built a Gurdwara to commemorate Guru Nanak Dev's visit. That Gurdwara still stands there, even though it was damaged in an earthquake in 1930.

28 *Guru Granth Sahib*, page 663.

Guru Nanak meets Rani Nur Shah in Assam.

In subsequent stanzas, the Guru goes on to describe how God is formless, yet seen through the forms of His creation. He asks for the blessing of God so as to enable him to reside at His feet.

After this, started the return journey. It meant a difficult trek through the jungles of Central India, where, for days on end, the Guru and his faithful companion, Mardana, did not come across any habitation. They were at the mercy of the elements and had to make do with whatever meagre food they carried and the pickings of various fruit and berries in the jungle.

On their way, near Lahore, they came to Kangarpur, where they were not treated well by the villagers. As they were leaving, the *janamsakhi* tradition tells us, the Guru said: "May you continue to prosper in this very village." Soon thereafter, they went to Manak, where they were welcomed warmly, and spent a night there. As they were leaving, the Guru said: "May this village be deserted."

When Mardana asked him about the seemingly inappropriate responses, the Guru said that negative attitude of the first village should be contained. On the other hand, if the warm and caring people of the second village were to spread out into the world, they would have a positive impact wherever they went and thus goodness would permeate the world through them.

The details about the return journey of Guru Nanak are somewhat sketchy, but we know that wherever he and Mardana went and met people, they would sing the praise of God and spread the message of universal brotherhood and love.

Pakpattan, which means 'the bank, or ferry of the pure one', was a principal town on the banks of River Sutlej. It was a major centre of commerce and housed an establishment of Sheikh Farid, the famous Sufi mystic.

Here Guru Nanak met Shaikh Ibrahim, who was a descendent of Sheikh Farid. The Guru and the Sheikh discussed their different ways of attaining the same goal, of attunement with God.

The Sufi mystic was typical of the time. He could not see how anyone could attain *moksha* without withdrawing from the world and without leading a life of denial and meditation. On the other hand, Guru Nanak maintained that one did not have to deny oneself, that true *moksha* could be attained if one could attune himself to the Will of God while living a life in which he carried out the duties assigned by family and society.

On their way home, as they neared Talwandi, Mardana became impatient and he asked the Guru for permission to hurry ahead, so as to meet his family. The family was overjoyed to see him after such a long time, and news of his return spread like wildfire. Soon Tripta, Guru Nanak's mother, rushed to the periphery of the village to meet her son, who touched her feet as a mark of respect. The Guru's father also soon reached the spot where his son was. It was time for the family to get together.

Guru Nanak stayed in Talwandi for a few days, and spent much time with Rai Bular, the local chieftain who had been his most vocal admirer when he was a young boy. Now Rai Bular had become old and frail. The two had much to discuss and share.

Guru Nanak then went to Sultanpur. His sister Nanaki and his brother-in-law Jai Ram were overjoyed to see him. His wife Sulakhni and children, Srichand and Lakhmidas, were all together again;

Sulakhni had just returned from her parents' home in Batala.

Even as he spent time with his family, the Guru continued to hold his congregations. His family life had been interrupted for 13 years[29]. Now at home, the recitation of daily compositions in praise of God and the congregations continued. They were to remain a constant feature of his life.

Guru Nanak visits his home to meet his wife Sulakhni and his sons Lakhmidas and Srichand.

29 Giani Gyan Singh puts the year of Guru Nanak's arrival in Sultanpur in the winter of 1509 in *Twarikh Guru Khalsa*.

THE SECOND JOURNEY:
A MAN OF GOD ONLY ADDS FRAGRANCE

"If you give in the name of God and put food into the mouths of needy persons, only then will you have credit to take with you in your next life,"

Guru Nanak spent some time with his family. Soon it was time to leave again and spread the word of God, now in a different direction. Setting forth from Sultanpur, he proceeded northwest, visiting Goindwal after crossing the River Beas. He went on from there to Lahore, where he had a significant encounter with Duni Chand, a rich merchant.

Duni Chand was performing the rites for the deceased. These rites associated with Hinduism include ritualistically offering food to Brahmins during the period of *shradh*. It is said that the food given to Brahmins during these days is an offering made to the departed souls of the ancestors and brings blessings to the dead.

The merchant's ostentatious display of wealth was for all to see, and he was especially proud of the seven flags that hung at his doorway signifying his wealth.

Guru Nanak taught his lesson in a simple way. He gave Duni Chand a needle and told him that he would take it from him in the next world. This made the merchant think and realise that he could not take any of his worldly possessions with him to a life after death. He asked for the Guru's advice about what to do with all his material wealth.

"If you give in the name of God and put food into the mouths of needy persons, only then will you have credit to take with you in your next life," replied Guru Nanak.

opposite page:
Guru Nanak's encounter with Raja Shivnabh.

Travelling further through Talwandi and Saidpur, Guru Nanak came to Sialkot, a town that traced its history to antiquity and was at one time the capital of Punjab. When Guru Nanak reached there, he found the populace under tremendous strain. A Sufi saint had announced that he would punish all the townspeople because one of them had broken a promise.

Ganga, a Kshatriya resident, had been childless for long. He had promised Hamaz Ghaus, the Sufi saint, that he would give his first child to the saint and make him a disciple of Hamaz Ghaus. Ganga had three sons subsequently, but he went back on his word. At this the saint got enraged and threatened to destroy the townspeople.

When Hamaz Ghaus emerged after forty days of penance to punish the promise breakers, Guru Nanak interceded on their behalf. "Those who have done no wrong should not be punished for the sin of one wrongdoer," he declared.

"But they are all liars," said the enraged Sufi.

"There must be some person here who is both truthful and wise," replied the Guru.

He gave Mardana two coins and asked him to go to the town and purchase truth worth a coin and falsehood worth the other. By now, Mardana was used to being sent out on seemingly strange errands. He proceeded to the town and visited many a shop asking for the goods that Guru Nanak had asked to be bought.

At one shop, Moola, the shopkeeper, took the coins from him and gave the answer in writing. "Life is a lie," he wrote on a slip. "Death is the truth," he wrote on another. When the answers were presented to Hamaz Ghaus, the saint saw that there were indeed some persons who did not deserve to die, and he decided not to punish the townspeople. Moola, who had followed Mardana to the Guru's presence after writing down the statements, became a disciple of Guru Nanak and took upon himself the task of spreading the Guru's word in the area. Here Guru Nanak had spent some time under the shade of a *beri* (a fruit tree). Gurdwara Ber Sahib now stands at the spot where the Guru sat in Sialkot, now in Pakistan.

The Guru then went to Bathinda where he stayed a while. Sirsa was the next major stop. This place is also important because it is one of the few where the date of his visit is firmly established—11 June 1510.[30] Here the Guru spent three months and interacted with the Sufis, who were said to be very powerful because of their occult practices. The Guru's response was to point out that compassion and piety were what made a saint great, not his powers.

From Sirsa, he journeyed on to Bikaner in the Thar Desert. This area was dominated by the ascetic Jains. They did not drink even water without straining it, lest some small insect be killed. Eating of fresh — and therefore living — grain was taboo to them, as were various other living things.

---

30 The date mentioned in *Twarikh Guru Khalsa* by Giani Gyan Singh is 14 Har 1597 Bikrami, which corresponds to this date.

When asked, the Guru responded by saying that he, like most people, ate fresh grain, fresh fruits and so on. He was warned by the Jains that he would never attain *moksha,* but the Guru replied that their worldview did not take into account the grace of God, which was essential to attaining *moksha*:

> By the Lord's grace desire is satiated;
> By the Lord's grace there is no sorrow;
> By the Lord's grace there is suffering;
> By the Lord's grace divine bliss is savoured;
> By the Lord's grace the fear of death is annulled;
> By the Lord's grace the body becomes healthy and fit;
> By the Lord's grace the nine treasures are obtained;
> By the Lord's grace Truth is realised. [31]

Guru Nanak then travelled to Ajmer and it was at the mausoleum of Khawaja Mu'in-ud-Din Chisti that he held discussions with members of the well-regarded Sufi order founded by the Sufi saint Chisti. Pushkar, where a famous camel festival is held every year now, was nearby, and Guru Nanak held discourses for the multitude that had assembled there for the festival of Baisakhi, the post-harvest festival.

Various *janamsakhi*s talk about Guru Nanak travelling all the way to Sri Lanka during this particular journey, but they do not give the details of the places he visited. In south India, Rameshwaram still has an old shrine called Nanak Udasi Math that marks the visit of the founder of the Sikh religion, and there are some other places also which are associated with him. Some early manuscripts have a chapter called *Haquiqat Rah Mukam Shivnabh Raje Ki,* which is, as tradition tells us, based on the account of Bhai Piara, a Sikh sent to Sri Lanka by the fifth Guru, Guru Arjan Dev, to get details of Guru Nanak's travels. Bhai Piara came back with a document called *Pransangali* which was compiled by Saido Jat, a scribe who had accompanied Guru Nanak. Guru Arjan Dev did not consider the version genuine, and, therefore, it was not included in *Guru Granth Sahib.*

31 *Guru Granth Sahib,* page 149.

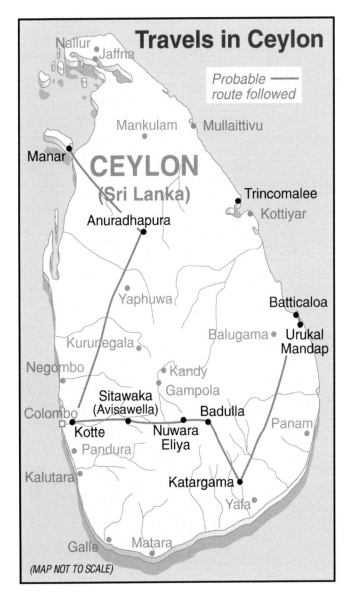

Going by traditional information, Guru Nanak met Raja Shivnabh, probably in the kingdom of Jaffna, which was one of the three kingdoms in Sri Lanka then. The Raja had heard about a follower of Guru Nanak, called Mansukh, who arose at the crack of dawn, bathed in cold water and recited *Japji*. He attended to his worldly duties as a merchant during the day. At night, he would sing *shabads*, or hymns, of *Gurbani* and did not have any idols in the house.

The Raja called him over and asked him about the absence of idols and his non-observation of the rituals associated with Hinduism. He further said that he had heard that the local Hindus treated Mansukh like an outcast. The man told the king of how he had become a follower of Guru Nanak and had given up following rituals. Impressed, the Raja said that he too wished to meet Guru Nanak one day. Mansukh replied that it would happen if the King truly desired it. The *janamsakhis* also record the interaction the Guru had with the Raja, and say that the Raja met the Guru and became his follower. He established a *dharamsaal* where *shabads* were sung in the praise of God every morning and evening, such as the following one of Guru Nanak which dwells on the mystery of existence:

Where does he go and where from he comes?
What gives birth to him and what is it that he merges into in the end?
How is he enmeshed and how is he released?
How is he subsumed with the Eternal
He who treasures the Name in his Heart
And repeats the Name on his lips;
He who dwells in the Name becomes free from attachment like the Lord
By the Lord's order he comes
By His order he departs
From ego he is born and from ego he stays
He who surrenders himself to God's Will is released and remains not in bondage
He meditates on the Word and practises the Name, finding deliverance
Like birds flocking to the trees at night,
Men come into the world
Some have a peaceful existence, while others live in distress.
Every morning and evening, their eyes wander over the skies
And they roam aimlessly trapped in the cycle of their deeds.
Those seeped in the Name regard this world
As a grazier's temporary hut in a rain-grown pasture.
The poisonous earthen vessel that contained their passions and anger is shattered
Without God's remembrance life is empty

opposite page:
Guru Nanak being received as a Guru at his parent's place.

The Guru's word dispels ignorance.
Man meets a revered soul if he is so destined
Those dedicated to Hari rejoice in truth
To His Will they submit their body and soul.
I, says Nanak, would touch the feet of such men.[32]

The Guru is also known to have gone to various centres of pilgrimage along the Western Ghats, though the details of the happenings there are not documented.

On his way back to Punjab, Guru Nanak had to traverse Rajputana again. It is in a town called Uch that there still exist certain items belonging to the Guru. These including stone bangles, a pair of wooden sandals, a stone mace and a wooden boat are preserved in the Toshakhana of Uch Sharif. There the Guru met a descendant of Sheikh Bukhari, a prominent Sufi saint, during his visit. The relics are treated with reverence by the descendents of the Sheikh.

When Guru Nanak reached Multan, the local *pirs,* or holy men,

Guru Nanak comes visiting at his sister, Nanaki's place.

gave him a bowl of milk which was full to the brim indicating that the town was already full of holy men and that it did not have space for another. The Guru took a jasmine flower and put it on the bowl of milk. The flower floated, without the milk spilling over. The traditional interpretation of this is that Guru Nanak had shown that one more man of God would only add to the fragrance of the garden. However, it can also be seen as saying that the milk of knowledge, if contained in a bowl, can go bad whereas the fragrance of knowledge, unfettered in any way, spreads far and wide.

Guru Nanak again met Shaikh Ibrahim at Pakpattan. The Shaikh greeted the Guru with great fervour and discussed the dichotomy of Hinduism and Islam with him.

> You say that there is One (God) alone and no one other besides him.
> God is One but there are two ways.
> Which shall one accept and which reject?
> The Hindus say the truth is with them and the Muslims say that it is with them.
> Who is right and who is wrong?

Replied Guru Nanak:

> There is one God and one way.
> Accept the One Lord and reject all else.

Guru Nanak continued on his way back to Talwandi, where he again met his parents—who had grown in years by then. He also called upon Rai Bular.

The local chieftain had been ailing for a while now and he wished to see Guru Nanak. This desire was fulfilled when the Guru went to his house and spent time conversing with him and preparing him for the inevitable. The Guru is said to have been with Rai Bular when he passed away in peace.

Guru Nanak then made his way to Sultanpur, to his family. The Guru's wife had been taking care of his sons who had grown to become strapping lads. His sister Nanaki and her husband Jai Ram greeted him with their customary warmth. Guru Nanak was back with the people who loved him. This was the year AD 1515.

THE THIRD JOURNEY:
OUR LORD AND MASTER IS SO BEAUTIFUL

...many would be moved by the simple and effective message that cut through the ritualism of religion, touching their souls deeply.

When the Guru left Sultanpur for the next leg of travels, he went northwards. He visited his wife's parents at Pakho ke Randhawa, and it was near here that he selected a spot for setting up a small commune across the river Ravi. Some farmers in the area pledged land for the new village, which was named Kartarpur, literally, the Abode of the Creator.[33]

The Guru stayed in Kartarpur for a few months. His disciples formed the nucleus of the population of the new village, to which he would eventually return near the last days of his life.

Accompanied by Mardana, Guru Nanak continued towards the Himalayas. He went to Sialkot and on to Jammu. He visited the Amarnath cave in the higher Himalayan ranges. Even in those times it was an important centre of pilgrimage for the Hindus.

Guru Nanak continued his journey, meeting people of all kinds and preaching the message of universal brotherhood and love. They would flock together for his morning and evening discourses, and many would be moved by the simple and effective message that cut through the ritualism of religion, touching their souls deeply.

33 This city is now called Kartarpur Ravi and Dehra Baba Nanak. It is now in Pakistan, just across the Ravi river and is visible from the Indian side. This town has many Gurdwaras associated with Guru Nanak.

opposite page:
Guru Nanak in conversation with holy men at Mount Sumer.

The clothes that the Guru wore made people curious, since he could not be slotted into any identifiable creed or sect. Guru Nanak wore a dress that was non-denominational. It was a practical composite of the attire sported by both Muslims and Hindus and what the ordinary people wore. Then there was the fact that Guru Nanak's constant companion during his travels was Mardana, a Muslim. This also surprised many.

Often, what he said would be in conflict with various established practices. He would engage in dialogue with those he met.

Puratan Janamsakhi narrates how one Brahm Das, who was proud of his learning, met the Guru and asked him who he was, what was the faith that he followed and what kind of food he ate. The answers to these questions would have enabled Brahm Das to place the Guru in a definable socio-religious pecking order.

To this the Guru replied:

> There is one path and one door, the Guru is the ladder to reach God
> Our Lord and Master is so beautiful, O Nanak; all comfort is in the Name of the True Lord.
> He created Himself; He is self-realising.
> Separating ether and earth, He has spread out His canopy of ether on earth.
> Without any pillars, He supports the sky, through the manifestation of His Shabad.
> Creating the sun and the moon, He infused His Light into them.
> He created the night and the day; Wondrous are His miraculous ways.
> He created the sacred places of pilgrimage, where people contemplate righteousness and Dharma, and take baths on special occasions.
> There is no other equal to You; how can we speak and describe You?
> You occupy the Eternal throne; all others come and go through reincarnation.[34]

Brahm Das became a follower and the Guru continued with his journey into the Lahaul valley. There are various places in the Lahaul and Spiti area that mark the travels of the Guru through the land of the Lamas. One such well-known spot is Gurdwara Pathar Sahib at Leh.

Towards the eastern side, in Sikkim, there is an interesting anecdote associated with the Guru's visit. There is a lake which used to freeze during winter, causing much hardship to the local populace. When the Guru went to the area, he was told of the problem. He took his staff and struck it at a certain spot. To this day,

Guru Nanak meets siddhs *at Sumer Parbat, which is now called Mt. Kailash.*

34 *Guru Granth Sahib*, page 1279.

the lake does not freeze at that particular spot. The place is known as Guru Dang Mareo—literally, the place that the Guru hit with his staff.

Local lamas attribute the cultivation of paddy here to Nanak Lama. *Nai mal,* a garland of 108 small lakes around a mountain in Sikkim, is said to have been created by the beads of Guru Nanak's *mala.* He is said to have uttered the words *"Balhari kudrat vasia,"* while seeped in the ecstasy of Lord's creation.

During his journey through the Himalayas, Guru Nanak also met the *siddhs,* or the ascetic *yogis.* They asked him about the state of affairs in the world they had forsaken. The Guru admonished them: "Darkness envelopes the world and the moon of Truth is not visible. Sin rules the earth and it is weighed down by injustice. The *siddhs* have taken to their mountain caves and escaped. Who will save humanity now? The rulers are impious, people mill around in ignorance." The details of this discussion are recorded in the *Sidh Goshat,* a composition in *Guru Granth Sahib.**

Even here, the Guru stressed on his fundamental teaching that forsaking the world, as the *siddhs* had done, was just taking an easy way out.

Guru Nanak made his way back to Sultanpur in 1518,[35] where his sister Nanaki lived. She had been waiting since long for her brother to return. She fell ill within two days of the Guru's arrival and passed away. Her husband, Jairam, died three days later. Thus two of the people Guru Nanak loved the most in the world left him within days of his arrival at Sultanpur.

Thereafter, Guru Nanak bade farewell to the city that had long been his home. Nawab Daulat Khan, who had given Guru Nanak his first and only job, also met the Guru before he left Sultanpur. This was their last meeting and the Guru continued his travels, this time towards the west.

*The Guru met the *siddhs* at Mount Sumer, now called Kailash mountain. According to some traditions Guru Nanak also visited Nepal and Tibet, where he is called Nanak Lama.
35 *Tawarikh Guru Khalsa,* by Giani Gyan Singh.

THE FOURTH JOURNEY:
DID YOU NOT FEEL COMPASSION, LORD?

Guru Nanak was dressed in blue this time and he mingled with the pilgrims.

The final journey that Guru Nanak undertook was also the longest. He went towards the west, eventually reaching Mecca, the holiest city of Islam. Guru Nanak was dressed in blue this time and he mingled with the pilgrims. As usual, he was accompanied by Mardana.

They first travelled in southwest Punjab through Multan and Sukkur, and went to Thatta, an ancient town near present-day Karachi in Pakistan. A building marks the spot in Hinglaj, a well-known holy site which is sacred to both the Muslims and the Hindus. Here took place a debate between him and some saints of the Vaishnavite faith, who, as others before them, were intrigued by the dress that the Guru wore.

Guru Nanak and Mardana then went along with a group of Muslim pilgrims who were on their way to Mecca. The party boarded a dhow, which was a small ship rigged with a large sail, a kind generally used by Arab sailors along the coasts of the Arabian Sea. They disembarked at Jeddah, the ancient port now in Saudi Arabia, and went overland to Mecca. In order to do this, they had to join a caravan that made its way through forty miles of uninhabited desert to Mecca.

The *janamsakhis* speak of the well-known incident associated with his visit to Mecca. As the Guru and his companion lay down to rest, they fell asleep, with their feet in the direction of the Kaaba. A Qazi, or a Muslim priest, admonished Guru Nanak. "How can you sleep with your feet towards the abode of God, the Kaaba," he said.

opposite page:
Guru Nanak in conversation with two Muslim holy men. Inscribed on verso are the words: Babaji Yuch gaye. *Babaji went to Uccha.*

"Kindly point out the direction in which God is not," was the reply the stunned Qazi got.

The Guru and Mardana also went to Madina, which is north of Mecca and the home of Prophet Mohammed. From there they travelled on to Baghdad.[36] Here, a carved stone marker commemorated his visit and later, a small gurdwara was built. It still stands today.[37] From Baghdad, the Guru made his way homeward, via Iran and Afghanistan, but details of these visits are not available.

It was on their way back that the encounter with Baba Wali of Kandhar took place. When the Guru and Mardana were near Hasan Abdal, Mardana went up a hill to get water from a spring near where the Muslim saint lived. Baba Wali, the saint, refused to give water when Mardana told him that he was accompanying a divine person. Said Baba Wali: "If he is so accomplished, let him find his own water."

When Mardana conveyed the message to the Guru, he was told to go again and request for water. Mardana again came back without success. Guru Nanak then asked him to remove a small stone from a nearby hill. Out poured water and Mardana soon had his fill. In the meantime, Baba Wali realised that the water in his spring was fast drying up. He was enraged and rolled a boulder down the hill. Guru Nanak raised his hand and stopped the boulder. A gurdwara, called Panja Sahib, in Pakistan marks the spot. A boulder with the impression of the Guru's palm is kept in the gurdwara.

opposite page:
A mulla chides Guru Nanak at Mecca for sleeping with his feet towards the holy place.

36 *Loyal Gazette*, Lahore, January 1918, has the translation of a tablet with the following inscription that was discovered in Baghdad. It says: "In memory of the Guru, the holy Baba Nanak, king of holy men, this monument has been rebuilt with the help of saints." The tablet dates AD 1520-1521.

37 The Gurdwara was damaged in 2003 during Gulf War II, and the Sikh community is making efforts to refurbish it and establish regular service there.

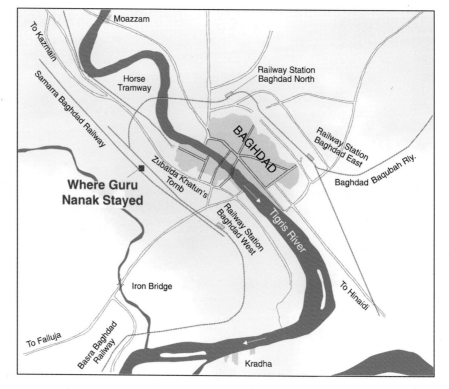

detail:
Guru Nanak visits Kabul, Afghanistan and makes disciples.

Guru Nanak was also witness to the plunder of Saidpur by the rampaging army of Babur, who invaded India at that time. Helpless townspeople could not defend themselves from the Mughal's plundering army, but they had resisted and for this defiance they were punished severely—many were killed, others captured and homes looted. It is said that Guru Nanak and Mardana were also captured.

The Guru expresses his anguish at the destruction that he saw in the following words:

Having protected Khurasan,[38] Babar terrorised Hindustan.

The Creator Himself cannot be blamed, but has sent the Mughal army as the messenger of death.

The tormented people's wails rent the air. Did You not feel compassion, Lord?

O Creator, You are the Master of all. If a powerful person strikes out against another equally powerful person, then the mind would feel little grief.

But if a powerful tiger attacks a flock of cattle and kills them, then its master must be called to account.

These dogs, the Lodhi rulers, have laid waste this priceless country and defiled it, now in their death, none shall remember them.

You Yourself unite, and You Yourself separate; such is the greatness of Your might.[39]

Guru Nanak during his imprisonment by Babur.

38 An eastern province of Iran bordering on the kingdom of Kabul, ruled by Babar.
39 *Guru Granth Sahib*, page 360.

How Guler painters envisioned Guru Nanak and his followers doing labour in Babur's prison.

The prisoners were told to do manual labour, of carrying loads and grinding corn with handmills. The Guru and Mardana too were assigned tasks, but soon the captors realised that Guru Nanak was no ordinary person and offered to release him. The Guru refused to leave if his other fellow prisoners were not released. This was done and Saidpur was restored to its original inhabitants.

It was now time for the Guru to settle down. He had spent many years travelling to most of the important holy places in India and West Asia. For him, it was now imperative to formalise his teachings and practices so that his followers would be able to lead a life in pursuit of God even as they carried on their daily activities.

ESTABLISHING A RELIGION

This was not a monastic order, but a lifestyle for the followers and an ideal society of God-oriented people.

"The Baba came to Kartarpur and laid aside the pilgrim's apparel. He clad himself in working clothes and continued the ministry even as he sat on a cot," says Bhai Gurdas, a very respected Sikh chronicler and interpreter, who was a contemporary of Guru Arjan Dev.

The morning would begin with the recitation of *Japji* and *singing of Asa di Vaar*, after which people would continue with their worldly duties. In the evening, *Sodhar* and *Aarti* were recited, says Bhai Gurdas.

This was, in effect, an idyllic setting for an ideal community, one in which Guru Nanak's teachings of equality, sharing, brotherhood, of helping one another and contributing to the life of the community as a whole were to be practised.

This was not a monastic order, but a lifestyle for the followers and an ideal society of God-oriented people. The Sikh tried to incorporate the Guru's ideals into their daily lifestyle. They also observed religious practices like the recitation of holy hymns.

Looking after his fledgling community was a busy time for Guru Nanak and his family. His parents were with him as was his wife Sulakhni and his sons Srichand and Lakhmidas. The family was finally together.

With the active support of Sulakhni, known to the Sikhs as Mata Sulakhni, Guru Nanak laid the framework of a casteless society by starting the institution called *langar*, or the free community kitchen that serves food to any and everyone. It would eventually have an enormous impact on how the Sikhs interacted with society.

By using the instrument of *langar*, Guru Nanak not only satiated the hunger of his followers, he also made them prepare food for

opposite page:
Guru Nanak with Followers and Other Holy Men. Opaque watercolour and gold on paper. Kashmir/Punjab, first quarter of the nineteenth century.

*Guru Nanak with Sadhus. Inscribed on
verso are the words: "Babaji setu Bandar
gay" in Devanagari and Gurmukhi scripts.*

everyone, sit and eat together. With this one act, he demolished the
differences of a society built on casteism. Even today in orthodox
Hindu homes, it is said the kitchen gets polluted if a person from a
lower caste steps in.

Everyone was expected to take part in preparing meals—
cleaning, cooking, serving and finally washing the utensils. Thus,
what were till then looked down upon as menial tasks, were elevated
to the level of service to the community.

It was at Kartarpur that Guru Nanak's parents passed away in
1522[40]. Baba Kalu was eighty-two. Within days, Mata Tripta too
passed away. The Guru took it stoically, as this was the Will of God.
Even though he had spent many decades travelling and spreading
the word of God, he was with them in the evening of their lives and
performed his duties as a son.

40 The year is quoted by Bhai Kahan
Singh in his encyclopaedia, *Mahankosh.*

Disciples of Jogi, Balnath, approach Guru Nanak. Inscribed on verso are the words: Sakhi chele Balnath de Mile. *The disciples of Jogi Balnath came to meet Guru Nanak.*

Kartarpur was now fast becoming a centre for the faithful. Sikhs from faraway places would come and gather in the presence of Guru Nanak, interact with each other and seek guidance from his presence.

Among those who came to Kartarpur was one Buddha, who came to be known as Baba Buddha in Sikh history. He was actually a twelve-year-old boy called Bura Randhawa, who belonged to a nearby village. When he came to meet Guru Nanak, Bura presented him a bowl of fresh milk. He said that it was indeed a great day for him since he was able to see the great Guru. "Please bless me so that I can get rid of this cycle of life and death," requested the young boy.

Guru Nanak asked him how he had come forth with this request in spite of his tender age. Bura replied that he had seen Mughal soldiers mow down ripe crops as well as unripe ones in order to set up a camp. That was when he felt that if no one could stop the soldiers, who could stop death?

As Bura conversed in the manner of an old man, the Guru said that he would henceforth be called 'Buddha', literally, elderly. Baba Buddha became a regular visitor to Kartarpur, and after a while he moved into the city of the Guru. The boy who thought of death so early in his life was to live up to a ripe old age of 125 and was to see the succession of five Gurus after Guru Nanak.

Kartarpur had become a centre of attraction for seekers of spirituality and people from all over came to meet the Guru. Among them was Lehna, who came from Khadur, a village that was sixty miles from Kartarpur. Lehna was a twenty-eight-year-old devotee of a goddess, and every year he led a party of devotees to the Jwalamukhi temple for pilgrimage.

During one of his journeys, he stopped at Kartarpur en route. Here he partook of *langar* and listened to *kirtan*, the recitation of holy hymns. He travelled no further.

Lehna devoted himself to the service of Guru Nanak and soon became a true and dedicated follower. He would clean the utensils after *langar*, a service that has been considered among the highest that a Sikh can do.

He had found what he had been seeking. In Guru Nanak's presence, he felt tranquil. What was for many others a chore, became for him the labour of love.

There is an interesting anecdote about Bhai Lehna. Wearing fine clothes, which had been sent by his in-laws, Lehna met Guru Nanak in the fields on the outskirts of Kartarpur. The Guru was cutting grass, which had to be carried to the village to be used as fodder. Lehna took the bundle of grass from Guru Nanak and placed it on his head, the conventional way of carrying such weight in rural areas.

Since the grass had come from a rice field, it was both wet and muddy. As Bhai Lehna carried the bundle, water and mud streaked his clothes. When he went to drop the bundle of grass at the Guru's house, Mata Sulakhni saw his condition and admonished the Guru for making Bhai Lehna carry such a bundle as he was dressed in fine clothes.

To this the Guru said that Bhai Lehna was not carrying a load of grass, but a wreath of sovereignty! The mud on his garments was as expensive and as rare as *kesar*. The Sikh lore is replete with anecdotes about the humility and devotion of Bhai Lehna.

A religious token depicting Guru Nanak with Mardana and Bala.

Another story is told of how a wall of the *dharamshala* in Kartarpur collapsed following incessant rain. Guru Nanak told his sons to repair the wall immediately. Since it was night time and both were feeling sleepy, Lakhmidas and Srichand said that they would repair the wall in the morning. But when Guru Nanak got down to repairing the wall himself, his sons joined him and soon the work was done.

Guru Nanak said that the wall had not been raised properly, and asked his sons to tear it down. They did as they were bid. But when the Guru asked them to re-build it once again, they protested and refused. Bhai Lehna, however, followed the Guru's command and continued to build the wall and tear it down again and again till Guru Nanak was finally satisfied. This story is often taken in an allegorical sense of Guru Nanak testing his sons as well as followers for total devotion to see who would be fit to carry on his mission after him.

At this stage, Guru Nanak was concerned about the question of succession as there was still a lot to be done for his mission to be complete. He had laid the foundation of a new egalitarian faith, and set up a nucleus of a regenerated society, but it still needed to be nurtured and guided; made stable and self-reliant.

Mardana, the Guru's constant companion, fell ill and the *janamsakhis* tell of how Guru Nanak was with Mardana when his end came. Reciting the holy verses, the Guru asked Mardana to concentrate on one God and accept His Will.*

For the Guru, it was a poignant moment. He had lost someone who had shared much of his life. Guru Nanak expressed his condolences to the family and asked them to accept the inevitable and the Will of God.

Mardana was ten years older than Guru Nanak. He has a special place in Sikh ethos and is the only Sikh disciple who was permitted to use Guru Nanak's name in his hymns. Barring the subsequent Sikh Gurus, he is the only person who used Guru Nank's name in his hymns. Guru Angad, for instance, addressed himself as Nanak II. However, Mardana is identified as "Mardana Nanak I". Three of Mardana's compositions are enshrined in *Guru Granth Sahib*.

Guru Nanak continued with his routine, but he had made up his mind that his sons were not competent enough to succeed him. Srichand was a person of great learning, but he had turned towards the path of renunciation and was becoming an ascetic, an *Udasi*.

Lakhmidas was interested a bit too much in worldly affairs and he kept himself occupied in material pursuits. Both were dutiful sons and good human beings, but the Guru felt that they did not have that which was necessary to qualify as his successor and did not conform to the requirements of pursuing his mission.

*Some traditions hold that Mardana had died earlier in Afghanistan. However, his death at Kartarpur is now generally accepted.

Guru Nanak visits Mardana's monument together with Bala and Mardana's son.

As Guru Nanak compiled *Japji* and *Asa di Var*, it was Bhai Lehna who assisted him in editing. The Guru saw in his devotion and piety a deep understanding of His Word. Guru Nanak thus chose Bhai Lehna as his successor as in him, he found the requisite qualities of piety, humility and devotion. He called him Angad, which literally means a part of oneself.

Puratan Janamsakhi has this account of the succession:

The Guru came to the bank of the Ravi. He placed five copper coins before Lehna and bowed down at his feet. Lehna, the faithful disciple, was thus installed Guru. Guru Nanak changed his own form and imparted his light to Lehna.

Guru Angad was asked to go to his native village, Khadur. As the news of the succession spread, the conclusion was obvious in the minds of the followers: Guru Nanak was preparing for his last journey. They began gathering in Kartarpur in large numbers. The Guru sat under a tree and meditated.

The family and followers were emotional and many were weeping. Guru Nanak asked them not to cry, since the Creator, who has assigned the world various tasks, sets the appointed hour at which the soul is captured and driven off. The body and the swan-soul are separated when one's days are past and done. One is rewarded according to one's actions and Destiny. He asked them to meditate and said that everyone has to pass this way. The false entanglements last for only a short while. [41]

The *janamsakhis* say that those assembled began to sing hymns of Guru Nanak and it was in this atmosphere that Guru Nanak handed over the manuscript in which his hymns had been recorded to Guru Angad, and took leave of this world. It was 7th September, 1539.[42] He was seventy.

Guru Nanak recognised the existence of one, all-pervasive God, and had spent a lifetime preaching universal brotherhood among the creations of this very formless God that had existed before time, God that is eternal, and whose creations we all are.

He also set up institutions that reduced the divisive and oppressive tendencies existing in society at that time. He practised what he preached, and by selecting his devoted follower and not his sons as his successor, he showed that merit alone should be the consideration in any selection. His followers were expected to live a life of piety, even as they carried on with their normal life. This is a tough choice to make, but it is the only one that grants success in both the worldly plane as well as that beyond.

41 Based on the composition in *Guru Granth Sahib*, page 579.
42 *Mahankosh* puts that date as September 22, 1539.

JAPJI, THE MORNING PRAYER

The Mulmantra *is taken as the essence of Sikh thought.*

Ik Oamkâr	There is one God
Sat(i) nâm	Eternal Truth is His Name
Kartâ purakh(u)	He is the Sole Creator
Nirbhau	He knoweth no fear;
Nirvair(u)	Is at enmity with no one
Akâl Murât	His Being is timeless and formless
Ajûnî	He is not incarnate
Saibhang	He is self-existent.
Gurparsâd	Attainable he is through the grace Of the Guru, The Enlightener.

Thus begins *Japji*, Guru Nanak's seminal composition. In fact, these lines are popularly called *Mulmantra,* though there is no such title in *Guru Granth Sahib.* It is considered the creedal, or formal statement of religious belief. Generally, the *Mulmantra* is taken as the essence of Sikh thought. The subsequent stanzas of *Japji* are said to be an exposition of the *Mulmantra* and the whole of *Guru Granth Sahib* a further elucidation of *Japji*.

Japji is a terse, epigrammatic composition of thirty-eight stanzas, or *pauris* (literally steps). It has two *slokas*, one at the beginning, the *Mulmantra,* and the other at the end. The composition is classical, using terms from Western Punjabi, Braj Bhasha, Sanskrit, Arabic and Persian. It is pithy and demonstrates a remarkable economy of expression. While the language used may be classical, the message remains contemporary, which contributes to its immense popularity.

Attempts to translate the text have seldom penetrated beyond the linguistic import of the expressions, though among the notable

opposite page:
Japji inscribed in Gurmukhi script so as to depict Guru Nanak as envisioned by Shan Pratap Salwans, Patiala, 1947.

A folio with silver foil decorative work (nakashi) from a 14 cm x 24 cm handwritten manuscript of Guru Granth Sahib *dated Samvat 1748 i.e. 1691 AD.*

exceptions is Vinoba Bhave's Hindi rendering. What is needed is to make an effort to intuitively grasp the true meaning of *Japji*. The following is a synopsis of the first five pauris of Japji.

Guru Nanak begins the composition by using the numerical 1. He is stressing on the oneness of God, on unity. That which exists can be quantified through numbers. Beyond nothingness is one. God is one. He is indivisible.

In a world fragmented by adherents of different faiths who believe that their God is the One, Guru Nanak says what is One can't be yours or mine, He is One for everyone.

What then is the essence of God? *Sat Nam,* or the Truth. There are many names for God, but the fact that Guru Nanak has chosen to emphasise 'Truth' as the defining characteristic is significant. In an age dominated by falsehood and deceit, what is most essential is truth. The pursuit of truth is the pursuit of God and, in this regard, philosophical enquiry and spiritual quest converge towards the same goal.

God is *Karta Purakh* the Creator. By asserting the role of God as Creator, Guru Nanak has taken a position that is different from that of traditional Indian spiritualism that held *Prakriti* (primal nature) as the creator. Here Guru Nanak distinguishes the Creator from His creation. The Creator is independent of His creation.

The Guru sees boundless love flowing from the Creator. He uses the terms *Nirbhau* and *Nirvair* to describe Him. With negative prefixes, these are words with a positive connotation—God is without fear, God has no enmity. Only one who is without fear and has no enmity can give boundless love. God's idiom is that of "love absolute".

God, as Guru Nanak describes Him, does not get annoyed, nor does He get angry. Someone who is angry can be appeased through gifts. But God never gets angry, so we don't need to appease Him. In any case, how can we even think of giving something to the One who has created everything? In addition, the mere act of giving is an assertion of identity, which feeds the ego, or *haumai*.

Thus, you do not appease God; you should attempt to merely live a life in which you follow His Will at all times and wait for His benovolence. Guru Nanak's followers must try to live without fear and bear no rancour against anyone. He wants them to maintain equilibrium between matters mundane and spiritual in their daily lives.

God is beyond the pale of time. He is timeless. He existed before time and will continue to exist after time. Here the earlier strand of God being different from His creation again comes forth. Creation is not eternal, the Creator is.

That which has been created certainly cannot fashion a likeness of the one who created it. Can a painting paint an artist? Can a pot shape the potter? No! Yet in each artwork or a pot, there is a reflection of the painter or the potter. God, who is *Nirgun*—one who defies all attributes—becomes *Sargun*—that which can be attributable. He is immanent and pervades the universe.

How exactly did God come into existence? Well, He did not. He is *Saibhang*, self created. Thus, all that exists came from Him, but He did not originate from anything. God is the Creator and the Enlightener and the Guru seeks His grace.

Meharban's *Janamsakhi* tells us that *Japji* was compiled at Kartarpur. Guru Nanak told Bhai Lehna to assist him. Like a jeweller and his assistant, the Guru and Bhai Lehna selected the thirty-eight *pauris* from the corpus of the Guru's compositions. These were then arranged in the present order.

As mentioned earlier, it is believed that during this endeavour, the grasp that Bhai Lehna showed of what Guru Nanak said and wrote, and his thorough devotion to God and the Guru, paved the way to his succession as the next Guru.

Colourful and delicate Kashmiri decorative motifs dominate a folio with gold foil decorative work (nakashi). *The 14 cm x 24 cm manuscript of* Guru Granth Sahib *handwritten on Kashmiri paper.*

The first *pauri* of *Japji* starts with the injunction *Jap* (to recite). Guru Nanak then says God is the originator of Time and Space. He has always been there in the past and will be there in the future. God is everywhere—on this planet, in the solar system, in distant galaxies.

How will we learn more about God? Meditation alone would

not help, even if one meditates a hundred thousand times. Contemplative silence would also not help, no matter how long it is. The path to realisation of God is such that even if all the possessions of the universe are given, they will still not be able to satiate desire without the contentment born of the true love of God. No intellect, no matter how highly developed, is enough to grasp it.

Then, how does one realise Truth? How does one shed the pall of falsehood? One has to learn to live by Divine Will, says Nanak. *Bhakti* is the devotional surrender to God's Will. One must, however, distinguish between *Sagun Bhakti* and *Nirgun Bhakti*. *Sagun Bhakti* is the devotion to gods in various forms, whereas *Nirgun Bhakti* is directed towards the essence of the Almighty, towards His Word.

Infinite are the forms that come into existence by His Will. It is by His Will that life continues and it is by His Will that we stand high or low. Only a blessed few will be delivered by His Will and only the one who perceives His Will shall be free of ego.

It is not possible to sing praises about His might, His gifts, His attributes, and His knowledge. Who can sing about Him, Who can take away life and bestow it too, Him who appears to be far, yet so near? How can the all-seeing and omnipotent God be described? Many have tried to provide descriptions, but have failed. His bounties are endless and through the ages He has always given to all creatures. He has set up the law of Creation, but He Himself is beyond it. He is beyond need and desire; He cannot be appeased, because He is never angry. Those who understand and remain in His Will are happy.

True is God and His name is uttered with endless love *(bhakti)*. He is the fountainhead of love and in order to approach Him and ask for His grace, one has to meditate on His name every morning, or, for that matter, at all times. Guru Nanak says that God can be neither installed, nor can His likeness be shaped. He exists by Himself and those who worship Him are honoured. Guru Nanak sings praises of Him who is the treasury of excellence. Only by singing and hearing His name and putting His love in our hearts will our sorrows be removed.

It is through the Guru's instructions that the Word is heard. Through the Guru we acquire knowledge and learn that God is contained in everything, everywhere. He cannot be described through mere words; He is the bestower of all living beings, of all life.

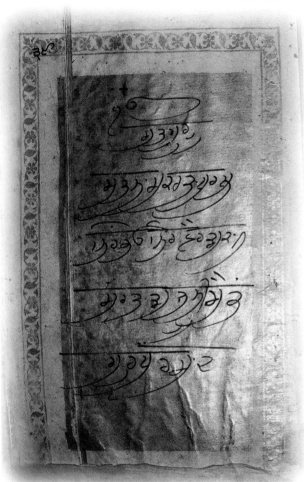

The first pauri of the Japji formed an important part of the manuscripts that had the nisan (handwriting, a signature) of the Sikh Guru's. This is a nisan of the Guru Tegh Bahadur, the 9th Guru.

We have summed up the first five *pauris* of *Japji*. If we take a closer look at *Japji*, we will see the following kinds of expositions in it: As explained earlier in this chapter, it starts with an elucidation of the concept of God in the *Mulmantra*. What follows is an examination of man's quest. The Divine Will is explained and then we find out about the path to God, that of *Nirgun Bhakti*, or worship through adoration. However, this is not possible without virtuous conduct. The human soul has to pass through five realms, or stages to merger, before the realisation of God can be attained and that too only through Divine Grace *(Nadar)*. Says Guru Nanak: "In all His Creation that I do behold, nothing, save through His Grace, avails".

In the *Mulmantra* and thereafter, the role of the Guru is stressed. The Guru is the Dispeller of Darkness; he is the God-conscious guide, the enlightened preceptor and a vital link between man and God. This should, however, not be taken to mean a personal Guru. For the Sikhs, *Gurbani* is taken as the Guru, since *Gurbani* is a revealed text.

Guru Nanak reaffirms and reiterates the humdrum reality of daily life in a positive manner. Many traditions treat temporal existence negatively; it has even been said that it is an illusion. This has led to a kind of despondence and lethargy among the general public, and a division between those who are spiritually inclined and those who tend to worldly affairs.

If the Creator has created the world Himself, how can it be an illusion? Spiritual existence is not for those who renounce the world, it is for everyone. Human life is a struggle for spiritual evolution, and at the low end is the existence that is governed by animal instincts. From this, man has to evolve to a stage where he attains the Ultimate Reality.

There are five realms *(khands)* of spiritual existence. These are the stages the seeker passes through. *Dharam Khand* is the realm where all creatures carry out their duties *(dharma)* in accordance with the Grand Plan of the Creator.

Gian Khand—the Realm of Knowledge. Here man's intellect is more keen and his mental horizons wider. He now begins to comprehend the basic unity behind Cosmic reality.

Saram Khand is the Realm of Spiritual Endeavour and it is in this realm that intuition, understanding and insight are forged. It is only through persistent spiritual endeavour that the human soul invokes grace of the Lord at the next stage.

Karam Khand is the Realm of Grace where spiritual powers alone prevail and here live only doughty spirits, whose mighty hearts

The illuminated folio of the manuscript of the Guru Granth Sahib at Takht Sri Harimandir Sahib, Patna, which has the nisan of Guru Gobind Singh, the 10ᵗʰ Guru.

A medallion with the Mul Mantra inscribed on it in the Gurmukhi script. Under it, written in Persian is the legend "Raja Darya Mal Devi Dayal Chowk Darbar, Amritsar. Made in Austria".

throb to the love of God. Here also abide such devotees who are wedded to Word Divine.

The final stage is *Sach Khand,* or the Realm of Truth, which is the *Nirankar's* abode. It is from this exalted seat that the True Lord watches His creation—countless orbs, regions and firmaments. These are sustained as He ordains. It is extremely difficult to describe how He watches His creation, how He rejoices and contemplates.

In the last *pauri* of *Japji,* Guru Nanak says that in order to purge oneself of the dross of ego, and shape oneself as He wills, let purity be the forge and have the patience of a goldsmith. Let Faith be the

A rather geometric rendering of the Japji from Guru Granth Sahib dated Samvat 1885 i.e. 1828 AD. The 13 cm x 30 cm manuscript is also called Lahori bir.

anvil and Knowledge the hammer. Let meditation fan the flame. Let Love act as the crucible and the Lord's name the catalyst. In this noble mint, coin a noble being of sterling mettle. Such is the lot of those upon whom Divine Grace has been endowed. Truly blessed is one upon whom falls the Lord's Grace.

Guru Nanak did not preach individualistic worship. Thus worship was not an individual's personal agenda. Any person's moral, spiritual and social progress is linked with the social group that nurtures him. Thus, worship and even the eventual goal of salvation are not to be treated as individual endeavours but as participatory practices.

We should never forget that Guru Nanak was deeply concerned with the ordinary man. Even in a composition as metaphysical as *Japji,* Guru Nanak laid down guiding principles for his followers on matters spiritual as well as social.

The last *sloka*, which is also found in *Majh di Var*, is by Guru Angad Dev. He says the Guru's word is as vital to the human soul as air is to the very being of Man. Water is the father (source of life) and the Earth the mother (sustainer), Day and Night are the nurses in whose lap mankind plays. One's deeds, both positive and negative, will be judged at the seat of the Almighty. It is these deeds through which each individual will be either drawn nearer to, or cast further away from the Almighty.

Those who have imbibed in their spirit His Name, their spiritually endowed glowing faces will redeem many more in their stride. The Guru again focuses on the search for God, which should be man's constant endeavour, since surely God has created us for more than mere physical existence. Man must continually try to evolve morally and spiritually and live life in accordance with His Will.

An illuminated folio with Japji *from a manuscript of* Guru Granth Sahib *dated Samvat 1963, i.e. 1906 AD.*

DISSOLVING DIFFERENCES: *SANGAT* AND *PANGAT*

Guru Nanak's religion is not for the individual alone; it is a way of life for a multicultural community that comprises people of all kinds. Guru Nanak sought to dissolve differences between the two distinct and mutually antagonistic religious groups—Hinduism and Islam.

In those days, intra-tradition and inter-religious interaction was rather restricted. However, Guru Nanak met everyone he could; he received education in the Hindu tradition as well as Islamic, made it a point to meet holy men from both persuasions and hold discussions with them. His closest friends were Bala, a Hindu, and Mardana, a Muslim.

The caste system was the bane of the Hindu society then, even as it is now. The society was divided into four castes—divided by accident of birth, not vocation or achievement — with the Brahmin, or the priest, occupying the highest position, the Kshatriya, or the warrior, being next, the Vaish, or the trading and tilling class, occupying the third place, and the Shudra, literally untouchable, coming at the bottom of the ladder.

Distinctions between various castes were observed strictly and intermixing was allowed between the top three castes only on the basis of strictly defined norms of social conduct. The Shudra's role was to serve the other three castes and even the shadow of a Shudra falling on a Brahmin was considered defiling.

Guru Nanak opposed the caste system vehemently. He says that we should know people by the Light illuminating them and (should) not ask for their castes, since in the world Hereafter, castes are not considered and no one is differentiated by his caste.[43]

⟨ornament⟩
43 *Guru Granth Sahib*, Page 142.

opposite page:
above: Sangat at the tercentenary celebrations of the Khalsa held at Anandpur Sahib in 1999.
below: Pangat, with devotees partaking of the langar, *at the Golden Temple complex, Amritsar.*

Preparing 2.5 tonnes of lentils requires dedication and devotion.

The caste system was so ingrained in the people that it was an uphill task to oppose it. Not only was the caste system exploitative and denigrating, it also robbed the ordinary people of their dignity and ensured the perpetuation of an unjust social order. Says Guru Nanak: "The caste of a person is what he does." At another point, he maintains: "The lowest among the low caste; those still lower and condemned—Nanak is by their side; he envies not the great of the world. Lord! Thy grace falls on the land where the poor are cherished."[44]

Inhibitions, superstitions and taboos fetter the functioning of the mind's freedom, making human beings lesser. In a composition in *Rag Sri*, Guru Nanak says: "There are the lowliest men among the low castes. Nanak, I shall go with them. What have I got to do with the great? God's grace comes on those who take care of the lowly."

The Guru "urged every man of faith to penetrate more deeply into his own traditions and find within them that core of moral and spiritual truth that is basic to all human religion. His call to transcend communal differences has stemmed from a deep sense of God and not an indifference to human religious effort. His concern was not with changing man from one religious community to the other. Nanak was concerned about the change from the superficial religion of ceremonial to a deeper religion of moral transformation."[45]

During his travels, Guru Nanak met many people who were converted to his way of thinking. They would be asked to hold regular *sangats* (getting together for a positive purpose). A *sangat* was not something new to the Indian tradition. History records that the famous Buddhist ruler Emperor Ashok had held large gatherings of Buddhists in order to discuss and dispense knowledge. Such gatherings were called *sangats* and were held at big towns, so that

44 ibid, page 15.
45 *Relevance of Nanak's Philosophy in Modern Age* by Donald G Sawe.

hundreds of people could gather and listen to the discourses.

Guru Nanak enlarged the concept. Instead of being held periodically, *sangat* became a daily congregational prayer in which Sikhs gathered to recite *Gurbani*. Says Guru Nanak: "*Satsangat* is one in which One Name is discussed." Elsewhere, he says: "In *sangat* God resides"

Thus, an atmosphere would be created in which people could gather and recite His name. Though the intent and the focus was spiritual, the *sangat* also operated at a temporal plane, since it was used to dissolve differences between members of the same society. If everyone sat together, they could not quite enforce "unsociability," the exclusion of the *shudras*.

Guru Nanak asserts that God does not mind our caste or birth, and he exhorts us to learn the way of truthful living, since it is our deeds that proclaim our caste and respect.[46]

When Guru Nanak set up Kartarpur, he made *sangat* a regular feature of the new city. A typical day at Kartarpur was structured around three daily prayers recited at sunrise, sunset and just before going to sleep. The first two prayers were recited by the Sikhs in a group whereas the last was recited individually.

The place where such a *sangat* was normally held was called a

---

46 *Guru Granth Sahib*, page 1330.

Given its size, the cauldron has to be cleaned in an unconventional manner.

dharamsal (the place of religion) and it was the precursor of gurdwaras. It is also interesting to note that even today, gurdwaras in Bihar, Bengal and Bangladesh are still known as Chhoti Sangat or Bari Sangat, i.e., small *sangat* or big *sangat*.

In medieval India, people did not eat together unless they were from the same caste, and of course from the same religion. The kind of food served also differed. Guru Nanak realised that social differences came into their sharpest focus in matters relating to eating together.

Those who came to these *sangats* were made to sit in a row

left: Everyone gets together to pray.
right: Modern means are also used to cook food at the langar.

(*pangat*) and eat together. This way perhaps one of the most potent taboos was broken down. It was a feat inconceivable in medieval India. It was a great leveller.

Traditionally, many religious places serve food to pilgrims. In fact, the community kitchen in the medieval Sufi *khanqas* was also known as the *langar*, which is a Persian word.

Guru Nanak organised the *langar* in order to feed the visitors as well as members of the community. He realised that hunger is a great leveller and demolished distinctions that had been artificially imposed on man by fellow beings.

The significance of *langar* has often been underestimated. For centuries, the Hindus, who constituted a vast majority of the Guru's followers, had been divided along caste lines. Now *sangat* and *langar* symbolised equality, fraternity and brotherhood. It is here that the high and the low, the rich and the poor, the learned and the ignorant, the king and the pauper, all shared the same food sitting together in one row.

Langar was run by contributions from followers of the faith, which could be in the form of provisions and/or voluntary service in preparing and serving the meals.

The *langar* offered two square meals to every visitor, especially

It is an honour to serve food at the langar.

to the destitute and the homeless, travellers and pilgrims.

Guru Nanak's mother, Mata Tripta, and his wife, Mata Sulakhni, were active in the *sewa* of *langar*. The important role of Mata Khivi, wife of Guru Angad, the second Guru, in distributing and supervising the preparation of food for *langar* is recorded by the bards Rai Baiwand and Satta, in *Guru Granth Sahib*. The prominence of *langar* in Sikh mindscape can be seen from the fact that during the 1783 *chalisa* famine that followed three consecutive failures of the monsoons, Sikh rulers and even landlords kept *langar* going. To cite an example, Budh Singh of Montgomery district sold off his property to pay for the food served to the needy.

Today, *langar* is an integral part of any Sikh congregation or gurdwara. The *langar* served to bystanders has become a distinctive feature during the annual Baisakhi parade in New York, Toronto, Stockton, or wherever in the world Sikhs reside.

At the Golden Temple in Amritsar, *langar* is now served in a separate building made for the purpose. It is served to tens of thousands of pilgrims every day, and to hundreds of thousands on festivals. Nowadays, food served in all *langars* is vegetarian.

SPEAKING OF WOMEN

The status of woman in the society that Guru Nanak lived in was that of an inferior—the property of man. Women were treated poorly, and were not much better off than servants. Without patriarchal protection in the form of a father or a husband, a woman was not considered respectable and was considered "fallen", meant for entertainment.

Thus, it was said there was pleasure in gold, pleasure in silver, pleasure in scents, pleasure in horses, pleasure in women, pleasure in conjugal bed, and so on. A woman was regarded as a distraction that entices a person away from the path of spiritualism.

While polygamy was common among the Hindus and Muslims, widow remarriage was not allowed, and, in fact, among some Hindus, women were expected to perform Sati, i.e., burn themselves at the pyre of their husband, since they had no life thereafter.

Child marriage and female infanticide were prevalent. Women were kept in veils.

It was in this world that Guru Nanak had the courage to say that women were worthy of praise and equal to men.

> From woman is man born
> Inside her is he conceived
> To woman is man engaged
> And woman he marries
> Woman is man's companion
> From woman come into being new generations
> Should a woman die, another is sought
> By woman's help is man kept in restraint
> Why revile her, of whom are born great ones of the earth? [47]

47 ibid, page 18.

opposite page:
Nanaki touches Guru Nanak's feet in reverence but Nanak stops her, since she is elder.

Guru Nanak, accompanied by Mardana, meets his sister, Nanaki.

Guru Nanak often uses the metaphor of a bride to describe the relationship of the seeker with the Lord. It must be stressed that while what he suggested was radical in its vision, the social system prevalent at the time was such that not much could be done for the emancipation of women.

However, he came out strongly against one of the most disingenuous devices used for subjugation. This was the notion of *sutak*, or impurity. In the Brahminical system, it was believed that any death rendered impure those of the household in which the demise had occurred. It also held that women, due to physiological differences, were most prone to such impurity, during childbirth, menstrual periods and so on. Guru Nanak condemned this notion in no uncertain terms:

Should *sutak* be believed in, then know that such impurity occurs everywhere.
Worms are found inside wood and cow dung.
No single grain of cereal is without life in it.
Water, which nurtures everything, is full of beings that live and die in it,

How may impurity of *sutak* be believed when it occurs even in the kitchen?

O Nanak, the impurity cannot be negated by anything other than enlightenment.[48]

Negating impurity, or *sutak*, is not a matter of curtailing the rights of others, it is having the ability to focus the senses in the right direction. This important message becomes clear when we read the next *sloka*:

The impurity of the mind is avarice,

That of the tongue, falsehood

The eyes become impure when they covet women and others' wealth

The ears are rendered impure when they listen to slander

Says Nanak, the souls of such beings are tied up and sent to hell.

All belief in *sutak* is an illusion

That induces man to worship objects other than God

Birth and death occur by Divine Ordinance

Beings come and go by Divine Will

All food and drink granted by God to creation is pure

Says Nanak, those who have realised the illusion of *sutak* have no use for it.

By encouraging the active participation of women as equal in worship of God, and in society, Guru Nanak created for them space within the prevalent patriarchal system. He attacked the very notion of women being inferior because of physiological differences. He took the notion of equality of women far beyond what had been done before him.

The lead given by Guru Nanak in recognising woman as the spiritual equal of man and in assigning a positive role for women in society was taken further by his successors. To start with, Sikh men and women ate together and prayed together. The Gurus themselves gave great importance to family life and to their women—mothers, wives and daughters—which had a demonstrative effect.

The contribution of Guru Angad Dev's wife, Bibi Khivi, to the langar has been documented. His daughter, Bibi Amro, was well-versed in the scriptures and she sang Guru Nanak's bani at congregations. Guru Amardas had been impressed by Bibi Amro's rendering of the *bani* even before he became a Sikh. After he became the third Guru, he consolidated the Sikh position regarding equality of women. He denounced *Sati*, and prohibited the *purdah* for women, according to which, women were hidden from men outside their own family, often by using a veil. He also laid great emphasis on *langar*, through which he demolished social prejudices. He appointed

Keeping the faith alive: A mother recites gurbani *to her daughter.*

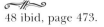

48 ibid, page 473.

Women are always enthusiastic in performing sewa.

women in prominent religious positions. Guru Amardas established 22 *manjis* (ecclesiastical districts) for men and 52 *peerahs* (sub-ecclesiastical districts)for women for preaching and spreading Sikhism. These were revolutionary steps at that time.

Manuscripts were prepared for the women family members of the Gurus, their genealogical details were recorded, which also point to the prominance of women during the time. Guru Teg Bahadur, the ninth Guru, named a town Chak Nanaki, after his mother. In Guru Gobind Singh's time, Mai Bhago led 40 Sikhs, who had once deserted the Guru, back into battle. The tenth Guru's wife, Mata Sahib Kaur, was by his side when he initiated the Khalsa in 1699. Sikh men and women alike became Khalsa. Mata Sundri led the Sikhs in the turbulent times that came after Guru Gobind Singh passed away. Sikh history is replete with examples of how women have risen to the occasion.

Sikh women have continued to make their mark since then. That they have done so in a cultural milieu that is hostile to women makes the achievement even more remarkable. Today you find Sikh women occupying a prominent place as scholars, poets, painters, entrepreneurs, political leaders, administrators, doctors and even police officers. Guru Nanak showed a new path for the emancipation of women. His successors broadened it. Building upon what was given to them in their religious heritage, which transcended the social limitations that still bedevil women, Sikh women now occupy prominent positions the world over.

EPILOGUE

Guru Nanak ensured the continuation of his mission by appointing Guru Angad Dev as his successor before he passed away. He had chosen his most meritorious follower, who had shown devotion and understanding, indeed, an intuitive grasp of the Guru's wish. In making this choice, Guru Nanak decided against the claims of his sons, Srichand and Lakhmidas.

The Guru had made a very powerful statement, by choosing his successor on the basis of merit instead of following the established custom, based on the principle of male primogeniture, according to which male heirs take precedence over daughters and the right of succession belongs to the eldest son. Though unconventional, the decision was entirely in sync with his teachings, deeds and precepts.

The word "Sikh" means a learner. The Sikhs went through a learning experience that included confrontation with various rulers and other trials and tribulations, even as they shared the eventual triumph of the Guru's vision.

After the passing away of Guru Nanak, his successors carried forward the mission of the founder of Sikhism for another two centuries. Nine Gurus, who were the successors of Guru Nanak, evolved, consolidated and institutionalised Sikhism.

Guru Angad Dev, who lived till the age of forty-eight, modified and codified the Gurmukhi script, and started a school at Khadur Sahib to teach the Gurmukhi alphabet to children during the thirteen years he was Guru.

His successor, Guru Amar Das, established twenty-two *Manjis*. The Sikhs had spread all over India. During his twenty-two years as Guru, he gave a fresh thrust to the institution of *langar*. When Emperor Akbar visited the Guru, he was asked to partake of *langar*. It was during this visit that, on the Guru's request, Emperor Akbar waived the *jazia* tax imposed upon non-Muslims. Guru Amar Das lived up to the age of ninety-five.

Different generations, united in faith. At the Harmandir Sahib, Amritsar.

Guru Ram Das, in a short span of seven years as Guru, founded the town of Amritsar and had the excavation of Amrit Sarovar, or pool of nectar, done at the Golden Temple in Amritsar. The Guru passed away at the age of forty-seven.

Guru Nank's compositions are unsparing in their criticism of the wrongs of social as well as political ills. The power of what he said was so great that the message of Guru Nanak and his successors was seen as a challenge to the political and social status quo. Confrontations were inevitable and with them came more visible signs of not only ideological but also physical conflict—you did not merely state the truth, stood up for it, too.

Guru Arjan Dev compiled *Adi Granth Sahib* in the year 1604. He institutionalised the concept of contributing one-tenth of the earning by the Sikhs for religious purposes. He started the construction of Harmandar Sahib and founded two cities, Kartarpur, which now falls in Jalandhar district of Punjab, and Sri Hargobindpur on the bank of the river Beas. The Guru was martyred at the age of forty-three, having been Guru for twenty-five years.

His successor, Guru Hargobind, donned on two swords, representing *Miri* and *Piri*, signifying temporal and spiritual power. He maintained an army and had the Akal Takht constructed. It

A sea of Sikhs that had converged for the tercentenary celebrations of the Khalsa held at Anandpur Sahib in 1999.

faces Harmandar Sahib, in Amritsar. The Sikhs fought four battles with the Mughals during the thirty-eight years he was Guru.

Guru Har Rai continued the tradition of his predecessor and maintained a cavalry though he did not engage in battles. His timely help to Dara Shikoh, the eldest son of Emperor Shahjahan, helped him to consolidate the community. He passed away at the age of thirty-two, to be succeeded by Guru Har Krishan, who was a child and also passed away at the age of eight, having been Guru for three years.

Guru Teg Bahadur, the youngest son of Guru Hargobind, was the ninth in succession. He travelled extensively in Punjab, writing and preaching Gurbani during the ten years he was Guru. His headquarters was Anandpur Sahib. Guru Teg Bahadur was martyred in Delhi on 1675, at the age of fifty-four.

The tenth Guru, Guru Gobind Singh transformed Sikhism and established the order of the Khalsa. The poet soldier left behind a large body of compositions. He was a patron of arts and fought many battles, sacrificing his four sons in the fight against the Mughals during the thirty-three years he was Guru. He passed away in 1708 at the age of forty-two.

What Guru Nanak had started more than two centuries ago had now matured and did not require a living Guru. Guru Gobind Singh declared, in Abchal Nagar, Hazur Sahib, in 1708 that the teachings contained in *Guru Granth Sahib* would guide the Sikhs and that there would be no living Guru henceforth.

Guru Granth Sahib is thus the Guru for the Sikhs now and is the focal point of the sacred and social occasions of the Sikhs.

Guru Nanak laid the foundation of a religion that continues to flourish, even as it has established itself all over the world.

Select Bibliography

G. S. Randhawa. *Guru Nanak's Japuji*. Guru Nanak Dev University, Amritsar. 1970.

W. Owen Cole and Piara Singh Sambhi. *The Sikhs: Their Religious Beliefs and Practices*. Vikas Publishing House, New Delhi. 1978.

Fauja Singh, Kirpal Singh. *Atlas: Travels of Guru Nanak*. Punjabi University, Patiala. 1976.

B N Goswamy. *Piety and Splendour: Sikh Heritage in Art*. National Museum, New Delhi 2000.

Ed: Harbans Singh. *Perspectives on Guru Nanak*. Punjabi University, Patiala. 1975

Gurinder Singh Mann. *Religions of the World: Sikhism*. Prentice Hall Inc., Upper Saddle River, NJ, USA. 2004

Surinder Singh. *Sikh Coinage: Symbol of Sikh Sovereignty*. Manohar, New Delhi. 2004.

J. S. Grewal. *Guru Nanak in History*. Panjab University, Chandigarh. 1969.

Giani Gurdit Singh. *Itihas Sri Guru Granth Sahib, Bhagat Bani Bhag*. Sahit Parkashan, Chandigarh. 2000.

Giani Gurdit Singh. *Itihas Sri Guru Granth Sahib, Mundavani*. Sahit Parkashan, Chandigarh. 2003.

Himadri Banerjee. *The Other Sikhs: A View from Eastern India*. Manohar, New Delhi. *2002*.

Harish Dhillon. *The Lives and Teachings of the Sikh Gurus*. UPSBD, New Delhi. 1977.

Picture Credits

Government Museum and Art Gallery, Chandigarh (Pages 4, 6, 9, 16, 17, 18, 20, 22, 26, 35, 36, 41, 42, 44, 48, 51, 53, 56, 57, 60, 78).

Sikandar Singh Bhayee (Pages 8, 10, 11, 14, 18, 19, 23, 28, 29, 31, 33, 46, 52, 76).

Giani Gurdit Singh's collection (Cover, Pages II, VIII, 66, 67, 69).

Chief Khalsa Diwan, Amritsar (Pages 64, 65, 68).

Himachal Pradesh Museum, Shimla (Page 54).

Sardarni Malwinder Kaur (Page 62).

Surinder Singh (Page 68 and back cover).

Baljit Singh (Page 79).

Pradeep Tiwari (Page 74).

United Sikhs (Page 80, 82).

Other photographs are by the author.